THE
LIFELINE

A HISTORY OF THE
ABERDEEN LIFEBOAT STATION 1925-1985

Norman Trewren

D1514513

£9.95

ISBN 0 9510738 0 X

Graphic Design – J.Sinclair
Printed by Gilcomston Litho (Aberdeen) Ltd.

Shell Expro is pleased to have been
able to assist in the production of this book,
which is being sold in aid of the RNLI

SHELL UK EXPLORATION AND PRODUCTION
1 Altens Farm Road, Nigg
Aberdeen AB9 2HY

*Shell Expro operates in the UK sector of the North Sea on behalf
of a 50/50 joint venture between Shell and Esso.*

Contents

Foreword

BY HIS ROYAL HIGHNESS THE PRINCE OF WALES

KENSINGTON PALACE

Norman Trewren has written a very readable account of the exploits of the Lifeboat service at Aberdeen. He covers all aspects of the work of an RNLI lifeboat that go to make up that great tradition of service to those in peril on the sea. His vivid account enables the reader to visualise what it is like to be with the Lifeboat and its crew while rescuing a family from across a flooded turnip field and to join them in an 80 hour period of duty at sea in unspeakably arduous conditions. Perhaps, more importantly, the book gathers together details of rescues and personal reminiscences which bring alive individual lifeboatmen's bravery as a valuable record for posterity. How often with the passage of time are such things forgotten and only belatedly researched as dull statistics long after the human participants have passed on and eye witness recollections lost for ever?

Our memories tend to be all too short to remember the days, not long since past, but before the advent of rescue helicopters, radar and sophisticated navigational aids, when trawlers returning to Aberdeen had to make a safe landfall by dead reckoning and then run the gauntlet of the harbour entrance with its treacherous bar and dangerous swell between the breakwaters, the conditions invariably made worse by the River Dee in spate. For those who came to grief it was only the professionalism and tenacity of the Lifeboatmen and the Coastguard Rocket Companies which lay between them and certain death.

Throughout this book there runs a thread of service and courage by Lifeboatmen in conflict with the elements. Although with the coming of the oil industry the face of Aberdeen has changed, these qualities remain as important today as when Coxswain Thomas Sinclair took the "William Roberts" to sea sixty years ago.

Charles.

Acknowledgements

The production of this History would not have been possible without the support and active co-operation of a great many people, local and national Companies and a wide variety of official Agencies. In particular I would acknowledge my indebtedness to the following organisations and individuals.

Shell UK Exploration and Production who generously defrayed the cost of the volume's printing and publication, as well as providing supporting services of many kinds; Aberdeen Journals Ltd, George Outram and Co., the Daily Record and the Daily Express for permission to use photographic and other items; the Imperial War Museum, Bristow Helicopters, British Airways Helicopters, BBC Aberdeen, the Hydrographer of the Navy and many others.

Coxswain George Flett, George Walker, Bill Cowper, Ian Jack, Albert Bird, John Allen and Mrs Thora Clegg, widow of former Coxswain Leo Clegg, provided much additional information over and above that recorded in Service Records and the media, while another former life-boatman, Jim Ferguson, was responsible for much research and also for editing my strained prose.

Peter Grant, Aberdeen City Librarian and Mrs Garden, Miss Taylor and Miss Deans of his Local Studies Department who cheerfully put up with a deal of disruption during the research phase and additionally suggested several profitable avenues of study.

Mr Roy Forbes-Morgan of Streatham for permission to use his hitherto unpublished photograph of "RNLB George and Elizabeth Gow" on wartime service in the Azores, Mr Patrick Lynch of North Star Fishing Company Ltd for the "David Ogilvie" photo, Mr Harry Peace, photographer of Aberdeen, and Mrs Shelley Griffiths of R.N.L.I. Headquarters, Poole, for her advice and provision of photographs.

At Shell Expro special thanks to John Moorhouse, Alan Jacobs, Jim Sinclair, Keith Murison and team, David Betts, Dave Stewart, Nora Park, Lorraine Smith and Sonia Hollands.

Finally I would like to thank my wife and family for their patience, living as they have for two and a half years with countless photographs, files and scribbled pieces of paper littering the house.

Norman D. Trewren
Aberdeen Life-boat Station
August, 1985

"Throw out the life-line across the dark wave,
There is a brother whom someone should save."

E.S. Ufford.

Introduction

In 1824, when Sir William Hillary, a Baronet from the Isle of Man, founded his "National Institution for the Preservation of Life from Shipwreck" with its aim of providing shore-based life-boat facilities around the British coastline, Aberdeen, like many other seaports, already had its own lifesaving service. This had been operational since 1802, although it was not until 1924, 100 years after the establishment of Hillary's organisation, that the harbour authorities formally requested the Royal National Life-boat Institution (as it had by then become), to take over their local station. In fact it is believed that Aberdeen's was the last major "private" life-boat station to be taken over.

For the first eight years of its initial existence the pre-RNLI service was managed by the port's Shipmasters' Society, but in 1810 the newly-established Aberdeen Harbour Commissioners took over responsibility for its operation. Until 1895 its finances came from a small tax levied on all ships using the port. In the main its life-boats, all of course oar-driven, were crewed by the Harbour Pilots, a highly-skilled group of seamen who lived in the tiny village of Footdee, hard by the northern side of the entrance channel.

But why Aberdeen? Why was there any need for a life-boat at this major Scottish port? The reasons are as valid today as they were at the beginning of the 19th Century — the Coastline runs approximately from north-east to south-west away from the city, with rocky cliffs to the south, and miles of gently-shelving beaches to the north. As a consequence the frequent onshore gales quickly transform this normally attractive stretch of coast into one of the most dangerous and treacherous elements to be faced by the seamen of any age — a lee shore. Many a proud ship has been driven on to these smiling sands, to stick fast, and all too often, to become a monument to tragedy until time and tide wash her away. Too many more have been dashed to pieces on the rocks bounding the port's southern approach, and the harbour entrance itself presents a considerable hazard in bad weather. Great seas can pound across its mouth, crashing over the South Breakwater, and in extreme conditions, even obscuring the light tower at its outer end. The entrance channel also serves as the mouth of the River Dee, and when this salmon fisherman's mecca is in full rain-driven spate, the strong ebb thus created can quickly generate disaster for any vessel unlucky enough to lose steering control during its approach.

In the 122 years of their existence, between 1802 and their incorporation into the RNLI organisation, Footdee-based life-boats lay claim to the rescue of well over 600 lives from all kinds of shipwreck. Whilst this cannot be accurately verified due to the sketchy, sometimes inaccurate, and occasionally contradictory press reports, there can be no doubt that several hundred 19th and early 20th Century seafarers must owe their lives to the men of the Footdee life-boats. The full story of this remarkable and gallant saga can be found in J L Duthie's well-researched book, "To the Rescue", published in 1981 by the Rainbow Press, of 171, Victoria Road, Torry, Aberdeen.

A brief outline of the events leading up to the RNLI's 1925 takeover of the Aberdeen station has to cover the growing concern expressed during the early 1920's over the city's life-boat capability. There was never any question of the skill and gallantry of crew members, but there was an awareness that their equipment was somewhat dated (for example, one of the two vessels had reportedly been built during the 1850's). It was felt that modern marine developments such as the internal combustion engine should be brought into the local rescue picture, but that funding for this major step forward was simply not available from local sources. Matters had not been helped by press reports of post-war operational difficulties, and when in late August, 1923 the RNLI, as part of a round-Britain demonstration tour, brought a brand-new motor life-boat to the port, the controversy boiled over once more. Obviously unwilling to become entangled in either side of the local argument, the visiting RNLI team contented themselves by doing no more than hint that, "it might be a good idea to have a motor boat for Aberdeen, and to keep their surf boat as well for emergencies".

MARVEL MOTOR LIFEBOAT CRUISES IN THE NORTH.

[" Press and Journal "
The **new motor** lifeboat, with the Aberdeen lifeboat Bon-Accord lying alongside for comparison.

Some six weeks later the trawler "Imperial Prince" went ashore near Belhevie, and although the efforts of the life-boat crew attracted the formal thanks of the Board of Trade, there seems to have been further concern over local rescue capabilities. As a result, the Harbour Commissioners, at their meeting on 12 November 1923, resolved to set up a sub-committee to look into, "the whole subject of the life-boat service at the Port, and the question of its transference to the Royal National Life-Boat Institution". By then the matter had even surfaced during the course of that year's municipal elections, when a questioner at a ward "heckling meeting" raised the subject. He was told that some 20 years previously a lady had bequeathed money, by then amounting to some £3,000, for the provision of a new life-boat for the port.

On 23 January, 1924, the local RNLI branch committee, strong supporters of the transfer theme, held a well-attended meeting in the Town House to celebrate the Institution's centenary. In his speech, Lord Provost William Meff said that for some time past, he and several of his colleagues had been urging the Harbour Commissioners to place their life-boat under full RNLI control. He was accordingly glad to be able to announce that matters had progressed to a level whereby a very early meeting between local interests and an RNLI delegation was to be held. This was greeted with enthusiastic applause, and other speakers were unanimous in looking forward to the eventual provision of the most modern and powerful type of motor life-boat, able to operate without restriction in the worst of local weather conditions.

The meeting in fact took place on 15 February 1924, and from it has stemmed the establishment and history of the present RNLI station. Matters must have moved rapidly as, at their meeting on 19 March, the Harbour Commissioners discussed a long letter from the RNLI, in which proposed conditions for the station's transfer were laid out.

Most of these need not concern us over 60 years later, but one still remains valid — this was the appointment of the Harbour-Master as the Honorary Superintendent of the station. Financial affairs were to be left to the Branch's Honorary Secretary, which arrangement still continues, and the Harbour Master is the present-day Launching Authority. As the year progressed, various other transfer-related matters were agreed by the Harbour Commissioners, together with a decision to provide £500 annually for the station's support. In addition to this the Harbour Commissioners were to provide life-boat moorings, shore facilities, and accommodation for the Surf (Number 2) Life-boat. All this took time, but the Footdee era drew to a close, and the RNLI took over on 1 January, 1925.

At this time the Harbour Commissioners turned over two rowing life-boats, all their gear, their accommodation, and no less than three sets of rocket line-throwing apparatus. This latter acquisition is believed to be unique in the Institution's annals, and is accordingly dealt with in more detail elsewhere. For their part the RNLI providing two temporary life-boats at the Aberdeen station (the first, a 34ft surf boat was first exercised on its tractor-drawn carriage on 9 January, 1925, and the second arrived not long after), until a better vessel for the beach could be provided, and a new 61ft Barnett-type motor life-boat constructed.

What now follows is the story of those RNLI life-boats, beginning with the two temporary vessels initially placed at the station, up to the present day ARUN-class boat and Inshore Life-boat.

Early Days – Star of the Wave

At 10.30pm on the night of 10 January 1926, the trawler "Star of the Wave", owned by the Walker Steam Trawling Company of Aberdeen, and homeward-bound with 70 boxes of fish, took the ground near the Belhelvie Coastguard lookout post. It was very cold and a thick haze obscured all shore lights. "Star of the Wave" was steaming into a moderate southerly gale when she stranded, and brought up all standing. Repeated efforts to free the casualty were to no avail, and the 205 ton vessel then began to take water on board. Seas were breaking right across the ship and her ten-man crew sought refuge in the wheelhouse and rigging, the former being constantly washed "up to the eyes" by the surf. The skipper, John McLeod, later reported that he repeatedly had to cover his nose and mouth with his hand to avoid swallowing water. All loose gear and fittings disappeared into the boiling sea. Then tragedy struck — to allow more room in the overcrowded wheelhouse for his mates the Chief Engineer, Nicholas Buchanan, made a dash to join those crewmen who had sought refuge in the rigging. He never reached this dubious safety as another huge wave smashed across the deck, and when it cleared he had vanished.

The remainder of the crew were by now in dire straits, but their continuous sounding of the vessel's foghorn, together with flares fired off into the mist, had alerted Coastguards manning the nearby lookout post. In a very short time Coast Rescue teams were called out, the pulling life-boat at Newburgh was alerted, and Captain Wyness, the Honorary Secretary of the recently-established RNLI station at Aberdeen, contacted by telephone. The Coastguard had very little information to pass on at this time — they knew that a vessel was in distress just offshore but had no idea as to its identity. All the first group of would-be rescuers, local farmers, found when they reached the shore was the body of Nicholas Buchanan, together with a faded and battered life-belt bearing the legend "Star of . . ."

In the meantime Captain Wyness had alerted the Aberdeen crew, and proceeded, together with his signalman, by road to the presumed scene of the incident. The Newburgh life-boat on its carriage was slowly taken southward along the shore towards Belhelvie. True to the conditions of the handover of the old Footdee Life-boat station, the RNLI had put in hand the construction of the new power-driven vessel for Aberdeen, but this was not yet complete, and earlier in January the two temporary life-boats had made the voyage from the institution's Poplar base. The first to arrive had been the "beach" life-boat "Robert and Ellen Robson", a 34ft by 8ft pulling boat made entirely from mahogany and fitted for ten oars. The temporary "Number 1" boat had arrived in the second week of January: The "William Roberts" was a 40ft by 11ft Watson pulling and sailing life-boat. A big boat, she displaced over 7 tons and mounted 12 oars. Built in 1903 at Thames Ironworks, Blackwall, London at a cost of £1,606, she bore the name of the Manchester man whose legacy had defrayed her cost. From 1903 to 1921 the "William Roberts" had been stationed at Littlehaven, and 1923-24 saw her based at Southend, before commencing her journey to Aberdeen. With a passage crew of just 2, the lifeboat had to be towed into Scarborough in a storm, her stores ruined and her complement suffering from mild exposure.

It was to this latter vessel that Coxswain Thomas Sinclair led his crew of 12 that January night and at 11.30pm under tow of the tug "Monarch", "William Roberts" set out on the new organisation's first service.

On arrival at Belhelvie it was soon apparent to Captain Wyness that the relatively deep-hulled "William Roberts" would be unable to approach the casualty to be of assistance. Nevertheless he decided to let his life-boat continue, and with the storm behind her, she arrived at about 1.30am, standing by despite the severity of the weather whilst other rescue attempts were made. In spite of their repeated efforts the Coast Rescue team were unable to reach the stranded trawler with their rocket lines, and the Newburgh life-boat was accordingly launched into the surf. It was swept within yards of the casualty, but due to heavy breaking seas was unable to make contact. At last a rocket line was held by the stranded trawlermen, and the nine

ABERDEEN TRAWLER WRECK THRILLS.

Wreck of the Star of the Wave, with the Newburgh lifeboat in the foreground.

The vessel that went aground at Bel-helvie, 11 miles north of Aberdeen, in a south-easterly gale on Sunday night, was the steam trawler Star of the Wave, belonging into her, and she was settling deep in the surf. A flare was lighted, and the siren blown repeatedly. Then it became a matter of "each man for himself." One half of the crew clambered into the Infirmary by District Officer Morrison, and his injury attended to.

Seen by a "Press and Journal" reporter after their rescue, the men made light of their trying experience, but all bo remaining survivors, cold, wet and totally exhausted by their ordeal, were brought ashore by breeches buoy.

At 4.30am, the recall signal was made to the "William Roberts", and thankfully Coxswain Sinclair and his crew turned for home. Their return trip, heading right into the storm, was accomplished (with the loss of two souwesters) by 6.45am, when they were again taken in tow by the "Monarch". This open-boat service had lasted some seven hours in atrocious conditions, but although they had rescued no-one, the Aberdeen crew did have the satisfaction of knowing that nine out of the ten men on board the casualty were safe, and that, as lifeboatmen, they had done what was required of them.

Launching the No.2 Lifeboat on its carriage.

R.N.L.B.`Emma Constance´

On taking over at Aberdeen, the RNLI debated long and hard over the choice of motor life-boat for their new station. They very obviously recognised the port's important role in the afloat rescue context, and determined to provide "the best that money can buy and science can devise". Their eventual decision was the despatch of a 61ft Barnett-type life-boat. She cost some £16,000 when built in 1926, this sum being met from a legacy left for the purpose by a Mr John Mackie of York. She was to be named "RNLB Emma Constance", and in the event remained on station at Aberdeen for some 25 years, serving as the "Aberdeen Number 1 Life-boat". The Beach life-boat, "Aberdeen Number 2", was named "RNLB Robert and Ellen Robson" and she remained in RNLI service, albeit not totally locally, until 1957. She is now on permanent exhibition at the RNLI Museum in Whitby.

Only three of these heavy (44½ ton) Barnett 61ft life-boats were built, and were the largest in the Institution's fleet. Even today their length is only surpassed by that of the 70ft Clyde-class cruising life-boats. The "Emma Constance" was 61 feet long, 15 feet in the beam, and her draught was over four feet. She was twin-screw, and powered by two RNLI DE6 petrol engines, each delivering 80 BHP. Her range at a cruising speed of nine knots was 200 miles, 150 miles at full speed of 9½ knots. The engines were each housed in separate compartments, these being included in the total of 14 watertight spaces throughout the vessel. She carried a total of 500 gallons of petrol, contained in three separate tanks abaft the engine rooms. An eight horse-power auxiliary petrol motor drove a generator for lighting purposes, and also provided power for a windlass forward and a capstan aft.

One of her most significant features was the specially-designed jumping net, supported forward between the two athwartships funnels and two stanchions somewhat further aft. The net was totally effective in operational service and although not adopted in any other RNLI class of vessel, can be seen today in the life-boats of the KNZHRM, the Dutch equivalent. Just how effective this net was can be gathered from the enthusiastic comments of one of the present Aberdeen crew members, who also remembers the "Emma Constance" with much affection. "The net? Och, it wiz fine. The men jumpit oot o' the casualty, intae the net, bounced oot intae the watter, and we ha'ed them oot from there!" The "Emma Constance", as can readily be seen from her photographs, was flush-decked, with shelters for the coxswain and the engine controls built on the main deck. The forward cabin was used mostly for survivors on return from service, whilst the after one contained the chartroom and, somewhat later, the radio installation. Although providing the latest "and best that science could devise", the

RNLI took no chances with the engines, going as far as supplying a full set of sails for the new vessel!

"Aberdeen on Saturday afternoon entered into formal possession of its new life-boat — said to be the finest and most up-to-date craft of its kind in existence . . ." So the Aberdeen "Press & Journal" began its large-scale coverage of "Emma Constance's" naming ceremony, held on 19 September 1927, and watched by between 10,000 and 12,000 people. After a brief morning shower, the Saturday weather turned fine for Lady Maud Carnegie, who performed the naming amid much display of bunting, speech-making, and brass band playing. The new life-boat was dressed overall for the occasion, and her crew were reported as looking "picturesque in navy reefers and scarlet knitted caps". The day's events ended, as has become a local tradition, with a brief cruise in the new vessel for the more important guests, together with a lifesaving demonstration.

"Have You Ever Been Out on the Lifeboat, Sir?"

If all the trips of the " Emma Constance " were as pleasant as that of Saturday afternoon on the placid water of the River Dee, there would be no difficulty in packing her with passengers up to the top of the funnels. This picture shows the lifeboat moored at the temporary jetty specially erected for the christening ceremony. A small tug is standing by. To the right is seen the moored barge on which the brass band of the 4th Gordon Highlanders discoursed appropriate music.

The brand-new "Emma Constance" on her arrival at Aberdeen harbour.

Late in the afternoon of 6 September, 1927, a dense fog accompanied by heavy rain covered the Aberdeen and Kincardine coasts, and the "Torry Orchestra" (the Girdleness foghorn) began its mournful symphony. A stiff south-easterly breeze soon built up a heavy breaking sea, and shortly before 10pm the Aberdeen trawler "Ben Torc", homeward bound from bunkering at Granton, went on to the rocks at Greg Ness about a mile from the harbour entrance. The surf soon turned the 198 ton vessel almost completely round, and she eventually came to uneasy rest with her bows pointing seawards. Green seas pounded over the forward part of the casualty, so bowler-hatted Skipper George Rose assembled his five-man crew in the wheelhouse. He also began sounding his siren, the continuous note of a vessel in distress mingling with that of the Girdleness foghorn, and help was soon on its way.

Coastguards manning the Greg Ness station scrambled down the cliffs to the scene, and, quickly assessing the situation decided it would be best to pass a line directly to the wreck. Two officers had to swim across a gully between the rocks to do this and after two attempts in which they were badly bruised the line was made fast. Perhaps unnerved by the Coastguards' experience the trawler's crew refused to have anything to do with the lifeline, and instead called for life-boat assistance. At 10.05pm, Captain Johnstone, the Assistant Harbour Master, passed the word for the life-boat crew to muster, and at 10.27pm the new 61ft Barnett motor life-boat ''Emma Constance'' put to sea. She had not been long on station, and in fact her official naming ceremony was planned for 19 September, still 13 days off!

ABERDEEN PRESS AND JOURNAL, THURSDAY, SEPTEMBER 8, 1927.

ABERDEEN TRAWLER WRECK AT GREGNESS.

The trawler Ben Torc, which ran on the rocks at Gregness Point during dense fog late   night. The cross shows the gully across which Coastguardsmen Davis and Fenn swam with a life-line to the vessel.

On reaching the scene of the stranding the life-boat's searchlight was used to illuminate the half-submerged rocks around the casualty, and Coxswain Tom Sinclair threaded his way through them to come alongside the wreck's starboard bow. The stricken trawler's five crewmen immediately leapt on board the life-boat, but Skipper Rose ended up in the sea, and had to catch a line. Once on the deck of the "Emma Constance" it was noted that the skipper was still wearing his bowler hat, despite his brief immersion. A life-boatman is reported to have said, "Look Skipper, ye must hardly have got wet, ye've still got yer hat on." Laying hands on the brim, he then attempted to remove the headgear, but the entire brim came away in his hands, the "bowl" remaining firmly jammed on its wearer's head!

With all six survivors safely on board, the life-boat backed out from between the rocks, returned to Aberdeen, and by midnight was back on her moorings. This had in fact been her second mission, as she had been called on 21 July 1927 to the aid of the trawler "Venetia" which was aground at Girdleness. Her assistance was not in the event required, so the "Ben Torc" service was another "first".

Early on the morning of 24 October, 1928, the Admiralty drifters "Lunar Bow" and "Noontide" departed from Invergordon to rendezvous with the controlled target vessel (converted battleship) HMS CENTURION at Portsmouth. It was a grey day, with a touch of oncoming winter in the air, and on rounding Kinnaird Head the two small 39 tonners soon ran into rising south-westerly winds and increasingly heavy seas. Lt Cdr Irvine, commanding the "Lunar Bow" accordingly decided to make for shelter at Peterhead, but this was frustrated by inability, due to the worsening weather, to make the starboard turn to enter harbour. He accordingly decided to continue on to Aberdeen.

In the "Lunar Bow's" tiny engine room Stoker Victor Moore had to grapple from handhold to handhold because of the violent motion and whilst carrying out a routine engine check at about 8.30pm, a particularly heavy lurch threw him into the machinery. His hand was trapped and badly mangled and the drifter had to heave-to whilst the injured rating was freed and then carried to his bunk. The long slog southward against the deteriorating weather was resumed, and although there was some slight lee off Aberdeen when the "Lunar Bow" reached the entrance during the small hours of the next day (25th), there was still enough sea running to make the approach hazardous. In the event, the Navymen were unable to hold their vessel on course as she shaped up for the harbour mouth, and she was swept away from the North Pier, coming to rest on the sand behind the Beach life-boat station.

In response to Verey light signals fired from the stranded vessel, the life-boat crew assembled and the "Emma Constance" slipped her mooring at 2.37am. After swinging round

R.N.L.B. "Emma Constance"

the North Pier she arrived within hailing distance of the drifter at 2.48am, and Coxswain Tom Sinclair was advised that a tug would be required for refloating purposes. More importantly, Stoker Moore urgently required hospital treatment for his injuries. Coxswain Sinclair swiftly made an assessment of the situation − it was then within two hours of low water, and with the ebb still running strongly he knew it would be impossible for the life-boat with its deep draught to come alongside the casualty. Bidding a temporary farewell to the stranded Navymen, he took the "Emma Constance" back to her moorings, and fifteen minutes later, at 4.15am, the Aberdeen Number 2 Life-boat "RNLB Robert and Ellen Robson", launched off the beach. She was manned by Coxswain Sinclair, his crew, and a number of local volunteers from the village. Within minutes she had come alongside the drifter. The injured stoker, plus a midshipman, were swiftly transferred to the life-boat, and on return to the beach both were put on board a waiting ambulance.

However the night was not yet over for the life-boatmen − by now it was 4.35am, and almost daylight as the "Robert and Ellen Robson" was rehoused. Coxswain Sinclair and his weary crew left the volunteers who had joined them in the pulling life-boat, and re-boarded the "Emma Constance". She slipped her mooring at 5.30am, and in company with the tug "St Machar", returned to the casualty. Twice during the course of the next three hours she ran in to the drifter with tow-lines until, at 8.30am, the tug's efforts were rewarded with success. During the tow into harbour it was discovered that the drifter had been damaged, and water was pouring in. At one point it rose above the level of the bunks in the after cabin, and the tug's skipper was accordingly advised to beach the drifter at Point Law, so that she could settle on an even keel. The fire brigade had in the meantime been alerted, and as soon as the casualty came alongside, their pumps were put to work. Once the flooding had been controlled the life-boat was released and returned to her moorings after a service which reflected the extreme flexibility of the local RNLI organisation.

The "Emma Constance" escorting HM Drifter Lunar Bow into port.

The Thirties

The crew of the steam trawler "John G Watson" of North Shields were happy — the fishing, some 140 miles ENE of Aberdeen had been good, and now they gratefully rested from their labours as their tough little ship battled homewards through strong SW winds and heavy seas. The time was about one o'clock on the morning of 22 January, 1930, and in addition to the stormy darkness, it was very cold. In his tiny wheelhouse, Skipper Thomas Patterson was not quite so content as a sixth sense told him that he was closer inshore than he should be, so much so that he stopped his ship to listen. It was too late. The "John G Watson" was already trapped between the two sandbanks which lie off the coast to the north of the Donmouth. From there, in the prevailing conditions of the weather and tide there was no possible escape. The 101 ton trawler took the ground with a jarring thump, its nine-man crew rushed on deck to join their skipper, and the night was soon lit by their distress flares. The vessel had in fact grounded near the Black Dog, some three miles north of the river mouth, just over six miles from the port. Her flares were quickly sighted by the Coastguard lookout on duty at Balgownie, and the local Coast Rescue Company was called out. Unable to reach the beach opposite the stranded trawler by road, they carried their heavy equipment for about a mile over the golf course and sand dunes, to set it up at the water's edge.

Meanwhile, Captain Wyness, the Aberdeen Life-boat's Hon Secretary, had also been alerted, and at 2.15am he passed the word for the crew to muster. The "Emma Constance" left her moorings at about 3.00am, and was in position off the wreck half an hour later. As Coxswain Tom Sinclair was away that night his place was taken by the young Bowman, Thomas Walker, and he was soon faced with a difficult decision. Should he attempt to cross the sandbank through the heavy breaking seas to the casualty in the deep-draught "Emma Constance", or would it be simpler and more effective to return to Aberdeen, bring the surf life-boat to the scene and launch from there? After quick, but careful consideration, Acting Coxswain Walker decided on the latter course as being the correct one in the circumstances, so he turned the Number 1 life-boat southwards, and headed back to Aberdeen. They arrived back in port at about 4.30am and reported to Captain Wyness, who immediately concurred with young Walker's assessment of the situation. The tractor drivers, launchers, helpers, and additional crew members were quickly roused, the big double doors of the beach shed flung back, and the Number 2 (pulling) life-boat "Robert and Ellen Robson" was trundled out of her shed. As many as could clambered on board the life-boat and Driver David Hoggins turned his tractor and trailer on to the Promenade, heading back towards the Bridge of Don. The going was good

The Thirties

at first, but once off the road the convoy had to take to the golf course, and then thread a path through the sand dunes. A difficult route, and one fraught with potential problems for David Hoggins at the wheel of the tractor.

During this time the casualty was gradually being driven to the northwards under the effect of wind and tide, and had moved about half a mile in the intervening three hours. A crowd had assembled on the beach, watching the stricken vessel when the shout went up, "Here comes the life-boat!". All attention was then turned on the tractor and its precious load as it moved slowly along the strand. Captain Wyness and the Assistant Harbour Master, Captain Johnson, had accompanied the convoy to the scene and they supervised the life-boat's positioning for its launch through the heavy surf. From the moment of leaving her trailer the "Robert & Ellen Robson" was tossed about like a cork — one moment she was out of sight in the trough, the next she perched high on the crest, bow and stern clear of the water, with oars seemingly flailing in the air, before crashing down to meet the next rearing sea. The young coxswain skilfully kept his boat's head into the sea, and manoeuvred her into the stranded vessel's lee at 7.55am. A rope was quickly thrown, and the ten men scrambled into the life-boat. The return to shore took only a few moments, and the "Robert & Ellen Robson" landed on the beach some 100 yards north of her launching site at 8.00am.

The actual rescue had taken exactly nine minutes, and was accomplished with the loss of three blue (port side) oars, two tins of chocolate — and two bottles of rum!

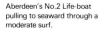

Aberdeen's No.2 Life-boat pulling to seaward through a moderate surf.

The trawler "Glenclova" aground on Aberdeen Beach after breaking adrift from her moorings.

From January 1930, until October 1931, Aberdeen's two life-boats carried out a total of 13 services, spending 24 hours and 25 minutes at sea. During this period one man was rescued — a fish porter, who tried to save the trawler "Glenclova" during the evening of 3 April 1930. The Dee was then in full spate, and four trawlers moored at Tilbury Wharf parted their lines. The fish porter, Robert Tawse, was passing the "Glenclova" at the time, and he leapt on board in a fruitless effort to make her fast. In the conditions his attempt failed, and the trawler with her unwilling passenger was driven across the tidal basin into the Navigation Channel. There was a stiff SW wind, and a heavy sea was breaking on to the beach.

As the "Glenclova" drifted past Pocra Quay the pilot cutter gave chase, and with Tawse's help a line was put on board. However this proved only sufficient to check the casualty's progress as she continued seawards on the ebb. Next on the scene was the tug "Chester", and at this point it was seen that the other three strays were by now drifting into the tidal basin. The tug kept on after the "Glenclova", which was by now abreast of the North Pier, still with the pilot cutter grimly hanging on. The trawler had swung round until she was broadside on to the pier and was bumping heavily against it as the strong tide took her down-channel.

Watched by a large crowd on the pier, Tawse attempted to gain access to the wheelhouse, but found it locked and had to take refuge in the rigging. The "Glenclova" eventually washed the length of the North Pier, rounded it, and quickly went ashore on the beach. The Number 2 life-boat, "Robert & Ellen Robson", was launched at 8.30pm and took Tawse off the casualty. Even then the drama was not over, for on its return to the shore, the life-boat was swept by a breaking sea. A crew member, George Caie, who was on his third service, was washed into the surf and the others at one time thought that he had gone under the boat and been drowned. He had in fact been able to grab the lifeline becketed round the gunwale, and once this was realised he was swiftly hauled to safety.

The Lowestoft drifter "Loyal Friend" went aground on the North Pier on the morning of June 2, 1931, and with her decks being continually swept by heavy seas running into the channel her 11 man crew were in some danger of being washed overboard. The life-boat was quickly launched, and on arrival found that six men had already been taken off by breeches buoy. The "Emma Constance", with Second Coxswain George Walker at the wheel, experienced great difficulty in coming alongside the casualty due to the profusion of nets and lines awash around her. Eventually she managed it, but much to the chagrin of her crew, the last remaining fisherman refused to board the life-boat.

Some time during the night of 1/2 January, 1933, the Aberdeen trawler "Venetia" went ashore some three miles north of Stonehaven. At the time a full Southerly gale was blowing, and the trawler was returning to her home port after a five day fishing trip with a crew of nine men. The wreck was spotted early the next morning by a farm labourer, but it was being smashed to pieces and no trace remained of her crew. At about 1.10pm the ''Emma Constance'' left the port and proceeded south, but it was soon realised that she could do nothing in the heavy on-shore seas and at 2.30pm, when off Findon Ness, she was recalled to her station. Her crew were unusually silent as the life-boat returned to port as, in addition to the knowledge that nine men had been drowned from the ''Venetia'', they felt a personal sense of loss. In 1927 the then brand-new ''Emma Constance'' had gone to the ''Venetia's'' assistance. On that occasion she was aground near Girdleness, but in the event she slid off the rocks and was towed into port by the tug ''Chester'', with the life-boat's services happily not being required.

Searchers found no survivors from the stranded trawler ''Venetia''.

A North-easterly gale, rough seas, and poor visibility welcomed the 18 man crew of the 2,000 ton Norwegian cargo vessel ''Granero'' as she approached the Scottish coast. It was a filthy night in October, 1933, and the freighter, bound from Finland to Grangemouth with pit props for the Lothian coal mines, was blinded by the weather, her navigation dependant upon dead reckoning. At about 7.30pm on 23 October she was slowly feeling her way south, when suddenly and quite without any warning, she struck heavily. There were three grinding crashes and then silence, save for the roar of the seas as they broke on the jagged rocks around her. The rain and mist then lifted briefly, and the Norwegians could see the lighthouse on Tod Head, together with the rocks all around their ship. The stricken vessel's engine was immediately put astern in an effort to drag her clear, but to no avail, and she was forced further ashore when it was stopped.

The ''Granero'' had gone ashore at Crawton Ness, some three miles south of Stonehaven, and a farmer, David Keith, who was walking along the clifftops was first to notice the wreck. He rushed to give the alarm and a maroon was fired to alert the local Coast Rescue Company. This was speedily mustered, and accompanied by a large crowd of sightseers, took its equipment to the scene. At the same time a call for assistance was passed by telephone to Aberdeen, and at 8.30pm Coxswain Tom Sinclair took the ''Emma Constance'' down channel. After rounding Girdleness, he turned onto a more southerly course, and increased to full speed

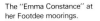

The ''Emma Constance'' at her Footdee moorings.

with the wind and sea behind him. In those pre-radio days all messages had to be passed visually, and as the life-boat passed Findon and Stonehaven, signal lights twinkled as updating information was passed from ashore. The Montrose life-boat was also launched at about this time, but she had to face the gale as she ploughed her way northwards.

The "Emma Constance" arrived on the scene at 11.30pm, and immediately closed to hailing distance of the wreck to ask if the Norwegian crew wished to abandon ship. "Not in the meantime", was the reply, so the life-boat retired into deeper water, and a message requesting tug assistance was passed to Aberdeen. The life-boat's powerful searchlight was used to illuminate the casualty, and in its beam the watchers, both afloat and ashore, saw the "Granero's" crew beginning to secure the breeches buoy line. The time was then about 2.00am, and shortly afterwards a tug arrived from Aberdeen in response to the earlier request. The Montrose life-boat also arrived, and after some discussion it was agreed that the tug would be of no use in the circumstances. It was released to return to Aberdeen.

The long night dragged on with the life-boats standing by offshore, to be told at 3.00am that 11 men had been taken off by breeches buoy and that seven still remained on board. At

The "Emma Constance" standing by the Norwegian cargo vessel "Granero" as she lies on the rocks near Stonehaven.

The Thirties

6.30pm, the "Emma Constance" again approached to within hailing distance, and the casualty was asked if the last seven men wished to leave. The Norwegians replied that they did not wish to leave, but asked that the life-boat remain on the scene. At 9.45am the life-boat was requested to come in and take men off, so Tom Sinclair cautiously went alongside and five more seamen were taken on board. The "Granero's" master, Captain Brandt, and his Chief Officer elected to stay, not wishing to leave their ship before dark. Just before "Emma Constance" pulled away, another 'survivor' was passed on board — this was the ship's mascot, a very frightened fox terrier.

The life-boat then proceeded to Stonehaven where the five Norwegians and their dog were all landed into the care of the authorities. A meal was provided for the tired life-boatmen before they once again put to sea, arriving back at Crawton Ness by 2.00pm. On their return they saw that the casualty had broken her back, so Coxswain Sinclair hailed her to ask when the Captain and Chief Officer were intending to leave. "Now," was the response, "But in my own boat!" An amazed life-boat crew then watched as the two Norwegians launched a small dinghy, and climbed on board.

It was quickly obvious that this last act of defiance against the sea was futile, for its two tired occupants were simply quite unable to manage the frail craft, so the life-boat moved in. The two seamen were taken on board, their dinghy was secured for towing, and the "Emma Constance" then returned to its station after a service lasting all of 19 hours.

Coastguardsmen on the clifftop at Crawton Ness.

The skipper of the Aberdeen trawler "Strathclova" anxiously bent closer to the radio, desperately trying to decipher the fragmentary voice coming through the roar of static. A voice he knew, even when distorted by the poor reception, as that of John Ballard, skipper of the "Strathclova's" sister ship, the "Strathebrie". The broken and incomplete text of the message was what had caused the anxiety, now so plain on his face. He was not sure of the exact position which the "Strathebrie" had been trying to pass, but Ballard's first four words were enough to cause serious concern. "Strathebrie" calling. Want Assistance . . ." Eventually the "Strathclova's" skipper thought he had most of the message through the terrible static, and in turn he started to transmit, "Heard Aberdeen trawler "Strathebrie" saying she is in need of assistance 80 miles NE x E ½E from Buchanness or Girdleness at 2.50pm; uncertain; difficult reception." As he transmitted, the skipper looked out of his tiny wheelhouse at the steep seas marching towards his own ship as she lay hove-to off Sumburgh Head in the gathering dusk of 21 January 1937, and he must have shivered as he thought of his friends and fellow seamen on board their sister vessel.

His message was picked up by the Cullercoats Radio Station in Northumberland, and retransmitted to Wick. At around 3.30pm the Hon Secretary of the Aberdeen life-boat was contacted by the Coastguard, and advised of the incident, together with details of the two positions received by the "Strathclova". Also passed on was information that Peterhead harbour was so badly affected by the strong SE gale and resultant high seas that no assistance could be provided from that port. Soon the cry was raised through the wind − and rainswept squares of Footdee, "Launch the Life-boat!", and men began to run. The "Emma Constance" cleared the harbour at 4.20pm, crashing through the breaking seas on the bar, and setting course for the nearer of the two positions, rolling heavily as she did so. Green seas and heavy spray constantly washed over her as she made her best speed in the prevailing weather − away into the night, and from her home port.

The trawlers "Computator" and "Neil MacKay" had by this time also reported hearing the "Strathebrie's" distress message, the former vessel being certain that she was in the same area, and about 85 miles NExE of Buchanness. However no further word was heard from the stricken vessel, and throughout the long winter night groups gathered at the Fishmarket to wait for news. The wireless station at the North Pier Pilot House from time to time intercepted terse messages from other ships joining in the search − the steamer "Bengore Head", the trawlers "Avonwater", "Sansonnet", and "Barbara Robb", but from the "Strathebrie" herself and the life-boat there was no word. In the latter case there could not be, for the life-boat, "the best that money could afford, and science could provide", still had no wireless.

The "Emma Constance" battled her way through the gale-lashed sea, arriving at the first position around 1.00am the next morning. After covering the area as best they could, her crew then carried on and searched the second area, but found nothing there either. It was a terrible night and there was no question of rest for the life-boat's crew. They could only hang on and peer with red, tired eyes across the tremendous seas, always searching for a trace of the casualty. Continuous rain and driving spray had reduced visibility to a bare minimum, so that the powerful searchlight could only probe out to a distance of some 500 to 600 yards at the most. Nothing was seen, and by about 5.00am all the possibilities were exhausted. Accordingly, with regret, and an utterly worn out crew, the "Emma Constance" turned for home. She now found it somewhat easier as the gale was on her quarter, and some four miles off Buchanness she came upon a Glasgow steamer, the first vessel she had seen since leaving Aberdeen the previous afternoon.

The life-boat was sighted from the shore as she battled southwards, and an anxious crowd of about 100 persons waited as she safely crossed the treacherous bar and finally entered port. Hope amongst the watchers, many of whom had relatives on board the missing "Strathebrie", quickly turned to despair as the weary life-boatmen, exhausted after their 25 hour mission, climbed alone to the quayside. They could only tell of their struggle with the wind, sea, and torrential rain; also of the dregs of fuel that were left in the "Emma Constance's" tanks after the long miles of constant danger. Of the "Strathebrie" itself there was still no sign.

Shortly after 5.00pm that evening, hope flared once again, and this soon turned to open rejoicing, for a message had been received from Buckie to say that the missing vessel had just limped into harbour there. Whilst some 80 miles NE x E ½E from Aberdeen she had been struck by two tremendous seas, one immediately after the other. The engine room was flooded to its fireboxes, the small boat was smashed, and the pumps were choked. For 14 hours her crew baled without a break to keep their little ship afloat, often up to their waists in freezing water. Gradually the level dropped, and the weather in its turn seemed to ease a little. Skipper Ballard was able to rest his exhausted crew for about two hours, but once more the water level rose, and he had to call them out again. This time they had to bail for some seven hours, and the trawler's safety was eventually assured. The "Strathebrie" had made some ground to the west-ward, and she arrived off Kinnaird Head around 5.00am on 22nd. This had been about the time the life-boat turned for home after her fruitless search, and some 12 hours later the trawler entered harbour at Buckie.

This long and arduous service resulted in considerable press comment regarding the need for the "Emma Constance" to carry wireless, and the matter was well summed up by Captain Wyness's report as Hon Secretary, "The service of 25 hours' duration was carried out under the worst possible conditions. Crew and life-boat had a most trying experience and great praise is due to the excellent manner in which this service was carried out. In my opinion a wireless telephone on the life-boat would have been most useful on a service of this kind."

Christmas Day or no, Aberdeen gave every evidence of its claim to be a premier fishing port as, throughout the 1935 holiday trawlers continually sailed from or entered the harbour. A stiff south-easterly wind was blowing across the entrance to the navigation channel, requiring caution to be exercised, but not sufficient to pose actual danger for the inward or outward passage of the several vessels using the port. There was however, a nasty run of secondary swell along the North Pier's inner edge.

The 141 ton Aberdeen trawler "George Stroud", owned by the Stroud Steam Fishing Company and skippered by James Phillips of Torry, was returning to her home port after filling her bunkers with coal at Methil. Her five man crew would have been eager to moor their vessel and join their respective families in the remainder of their Christmas celebrations. As is so often the case at that season it was a totally dark night, the sea merging with the sky to give a barely-visible horizon, and the lights of the ships in the Bay were twinkiling like diamonds against the black backdrop to the eastward. Shortly after 8.00pm the harbour lookout on duty in the Round-house at Footdee saw a tiny and multi-coloured cluster detach itself from the others to seaward, and shape up for the entrance to the navigation channel. This was the "George Stroud" and the tragic events of the next few minutes were about to end the city's Christmas festivities for that year.

Slowly her lights came on, until before the eyes of the horrified lookout, a huge sea rose up astern of the trawler, and flung her well to starboard of her intended course. Before her helmsman was able to take any form of corrective action, the heavy run of swell had thrown the stricken vessel against the North Pier. The little ship was immediately helpless, slithering and bumping as she was washed further along the ledge until she came to an uneasy rest, with a heavy list, and about 200 yards from the seaward end of the pier. The Roundhouse lookout, although shocked by the speed of the disaster which had unfolded in front of him, reacted with commendable swiftness. He telephoned for the men of the North Pier Lifesaving Apparatus Brigade, and also notified Captain Wyness, the Harbour Master and Hon Secretary, that the life-boat was required immediately. Only seven minutes later the lights of the "Emma Constance" were seen as she rounded the corner of Pocra Quay, and made her best speed towards the wreck.

In the meantime willing hands were hoisting a motor car on to the pier wall so that its lights could provide illumination for the LSA crew. As this was done the life-boat arrived, and it was seen that four of the trawler's crew had taken refuge in the wheelhouse from the breaking seas which swept right over the casualty. Although the LSA crew quickly established a link with a number of rocket lines, the trawlermen seemed unwilling or unable to leave their frail shelter to take hold of the means of rescue. "Give us the life-boat!" was their cry.

Coxswain Tom Sinclair swiftly weighed up the situation — he would have to bring the life-boat right into the broken water over the ledge, and then lie between the wreck and the North Pier itself. However, when the "Emma Constance" forced her way alongside, the casualty's crew made no move to board her. Time and again the coxswain and his crew shouted for the trawlermen to jump, but there was still no movement from the spray-lashed wheelhouse. The life-boat at this time was herself washed onto the ledge, lying there until the next swell broke over and around her, and washed her clear. Yet another approach was made, and this time the sea washed the "Emma Constance" some 100 feet along the pier before her Coxswain was able to bring her under control again. Returning again to the casualty, the life-boatmen saw a red pinpoint of light in her galley. As Coxswain Sinclair drove his increasingly-battered command up to the wreck once more, the Bowman, Thomas Walker, saw that the light was actually from a cigarette held by the "George Stroud's" cook, Sandy Wood. The life-boat crashed alongside, Walker reached out across the narrow gap, and grabbing the trawlerman by the lapels of his coat, hauled him bodily to safety in the few moments before the next sea washed the two hulls apart.

At about this time the Coxswain became aware that his life-boat's starboard propellor was fouled, and the crew quickly attempted to clear it. In the meantime, the men remaining on board the wave-lashed "George Stroud" had taken hold of a rocket line from the pier, but they were for some reason still reluctant to haul in the heavier rope with the actual breeches buoy. Again they were heard to shout for the life-boat. The "Emma Constance" accordingly came in once more, this time on only the one engine, and once more she crashed alongside the wreck. Again, no-one boarded her, and the next swell washed her clear. Shaping up for a further attempt, the life-boat's searchlight was switched on and trained towards the stranded trawler. At this point many of the silent crowd, men and women alike, wept openly, for the top of the ''George Stroud's'' wheelhouse had gone, swept away by the sea. Despite their horror at the suddenness of the tragedy, the life-boat crew came in again with their damaged vessel, and this time they saw a man clinging to the shattered timbers of the crushed wheelhouse. They also saw a man in the water, but although a line was quickly thrown and he grasped it, he had gone by the time the next sea crashed past.

The man in the smashed wheelhouse, the last survivor, was luckier, for spurred to renewed efforts the LSA team laid a line right over him. Weakly he made it fast, the breeches buoy gear was rigged, and he was hauled ashore to safety within a few moments. For a further long hour the ''Emma Constance'', limping through the heavy seas in the channel on the one engine and with her port side smashed, continued to search. Her searchlight probed the dark, but without success, and it soon became evident that there could be no further survivors. Two of the vessel's five man crew were, thanks to the persistent efforts of the LSA and life-boat crews, safe, but three seamen had also died that Christmas night.

In recognition of his gallant efforts to rescue the crew of the ''George Stroud'', the RNLI awarded Coxswain Tom Sinclair their Bronze Medal, the first such to come to the Aberdeen station.

The wreck of the trawler ''George Stroud'' lying off the North Pier.

The bad weather of late December 1935 continued well into the following month, and on the North Pier the wreck of the "George Stroud" also lingered on as a grim reminder of the Christmas tragedy. The hulk shifted continually, and the harbour authorities were concerned that it would slide into the navigation channel. Considerable disruption was in fact caused by its presence as entry and departure to and from the harbour was restricted to a period around high water, with the port being closed at night. Two lighted Dan buoys were also secured to the wreck in case any vessel might decide to enter the harbour against the "Port Closed" signals — an offence not totally unknown amongst Aberdeen fisher folk!

During the late afternoon of 17 January, 1936, the Aberdeen Pilot Cutter "William Porter" proceeded down the channel to change the lights on the buoys. On board were two harbour pilots, James Johnstone, and Andrew Patterson, as well as her mechanic, Bert Esson. The latter was a close friend of life-boatmen George Flett (who was eventually to take over as Coxswain from Tom Sinclair), and was himself a long-serving member of "the boat's" crew. A heavy swell was running in the area of the wreck, and a strong ENE wind was blowing flakes of snow into the faces of the pilot cutter's crew as they approached. Because of this it was difficult for the helmsman to hold the little cutter in place whilst the others attempted to change the eastern buoy's light. There was a sudden surge and the buoy mooring wire fouled the "William Porter's" propellor, totally immobilising the craft. The next swell lifted the cutter on to the remains of the "George Stroud", and the trawler's gallows smashed through the after part of the frail wooden hull. Forced clear by the next swell, she was washed right across the wreck, water pouring through the gash in her timbers, and she eventually came to rest by the focs'le. Her three occupants, quickly realising their precarious position, and fearing that their crippled craft was about to sink beneath them, made a leap for the focs'le as it protruded like a desolate rock from the breaking seas. They managed to push the cutter clear of the wreckage to prevent any further damage before, half-frozen and soaked to the skin, they sat down to wait for rescue.

This was not long in coming: as on that tragic Christmas night only some three weeks previously, the Roundhouse watchman had seen the drama unfold before his eyes. He quickly alerted the LSA Rocket Brigade, and also called out the life-boat. The "Emma Constance" was on the scene within only 15 minutes, and after some complicated manoeuvring through the heavy and confused run of sea, was able to come close enough for the three men to jump to safety. Coxswain Sinclair then went alongside the sinking cutter, a life-boatman leapt on board, and a towline was rapidly made fast. With the "William Porter" still making water and beginning to settle by the stern, the "Emma Constance" made her way into harbour and beached the damaged vessel beside the (now removed) dock gates near the present life-boat's berth. Three more men had been rescued from the trawler, which had taken the lives of three of her crew less than a month previously.

The River Dee had flooded his house before, and it had also cut him off before, so Mr James Yule of Waterside Farm was not unduly concerned as he went to his bed on the night of Sunday, 24 January 1937. The farm lay about a mile above the old Bridge of Dee on the river's south bank, and was reached by a narrow track, some quarter of a mile through the fields, from the main road. All the previous day, and all that day, the rain had poured steadily down, accompanied by a fearsome South-south-easterly gale that howled around the lonely little farmhouse. By 9.00pm Mr Yule, Miss Massie his housekeeper, and Mr Wm Alexander his horseman, were completely cut off by the still-rising river.

All over the North-east that weekend rivers had risen and burst their banks — the Don, Ythan, Urie and Deveron — with much consequent havoc in low-lying areas. Many roads and bridges had also suffered damage, with 30 houses flooded at Ballater, Riverside Road in Aberdeen closed to all traffic, and some 50 sheep drowned near Culter. Aberdeen Harbour, too, had its problems, with the gale closing the port to all shipping.

The little group at Waterside Farm had next to no sleep that late-January night, as by 5.00am the water was lapping at the back door. Experience dictated that this was the time to start moving the furniture upstairs, past the white-painted line on the stairs which marked the upper limit of the last great flood in 1920. An hour later there were some three feet of water in the kitchen, and as the morning wore on people on the South Deeside Road began to worry about the safety of the farm's occupants. The police were accordingly informed, and at 10.45am they decided to request the services of the Beach Life-boat.

At 11.00am that stormy Monday morning the life-boat "Robert & Ellen Robson" was launched on service from Footdee — on this unique occasion not into the North Sea, but into York Street. High on her trailer behind the big caterpillar tractor, she proceeded along the quayside to South Market Street, then across the Victoria Bridge into Torry, and via Menzies Road and Abbotswell Road to the South Deeside Road. Coxswain George Flett and his nine-man crew hung on as best they could as the life-boat and its carriage bumped and swayed along the last stages of the journey to the farm road turn-off. A large crowd had meanwhile gathered, with over 60 cars lining the winding road, where the convoy eventually stopped to survey the scene. A truly amazing sight met their eyes — there was an estimated depth of 15 feet in the river at that point, and it was running at some 10 knots, with trees, dead sheep, and much other debris being whirled seawards in the bilious-coloured spate.

The "Robert & Ellen Robson" during the Waterside Farm service.

It was immediately obvious to Coxswain Flett that the speed of the current totally prevented his oarsmen from rowing directly to the farmhouse, so the tractor resumed its journey, and proceeded another quarter of a mile or so upstream. It took 25 minutes more to manoeuvre the cumbersome trailer with its heavy load into a suitable position for launching. Even so a dyke had to be partly demolished before she slid into the boiling flood, floating well clear of what had until a short time previously been a ploughed field. Every move of the operation had been watched by the crowd, growing ever-larger in numbers, and loud cheers greeted the actual moment of launch.

The life-boatmen had to negotiate fences, outhouses and hayricks as their craft sped along on its alien element. Some 30 yards upstream of the farmhouse the anchor was dropped to slow the boat's headlong dash, and it took a further half-hour to reach the actual front door. By this time the flood had risen until it was buffeting the bedroom windows on the first floor, and the 1920 tidemark on the stairs had long since been submerged under a further 21 inches of floodwater.

A face appeared at the bedroom window, which was then opened, and a somewhat plaintive voice enquired of the Coxswain, "Why did ye no' come by the river?" George Flett looked non-plussed, checking over both sides of the life-boat, "I thocht this was the river, what's that . . . ?" he queried. "You're right in my neep field!" was the farmer's response. Two life-boatmen struggled to the house with a rope, and a ladder was laid from their boat to the window. There was then an unexpected delay — what was going on? Ashore an air of impatience grew, and a message was accordingly semaphored across the flooded fields to the life-boat, "Are you taking them off now?" A smile was evident on George Flett's face as he raised his arms and replied, "Not until we milk the cow." When this domestic chore was completed, the farm's marooned occupants boarded the "Robert and Ellen Robson", first Miss Massie, with a collie, then Mr Alexander, and lastly, with many a backward glance, the farmer himself. "I hope it won't be long before we can get back." he said.

The life-boat let go from its unusual mooring point and swiftly rowed back to the bank where its passengers were disembarked. After recovering their boat, and retracing their long journey from Footdee, the crew found that the "Emma Constance" had also been on service during their absence. This was to the fishing vessel "Utility", which hung up by its stern moorings within the harbour.

She was successfully cleared, and then towed to the Fish-market, but all were in agreement that the Beach Life-boat's rescue had been the most unusual of any service performed by the Aberdeen station.

The "Emma Constance" leaving harbour on exercise.

Bound for Aberdeen, the 249 gross ton collier "Fairy" of Kings Lynn, sailed from Goole on her fateful voyage on Saturday, 23 January, 1937. She was under the command of Captain George Croxford, with some 16 years' service on board, and as she steamed northwards a whole South-easterly gale made her passage extremely unpleasant indeed. Late on the afternoon of the next day she arrived off Aberdeen, but found that enormous seas were being driven across the harbour entrance by the gale, and the port was closed to all traffic.

Wearily, as if somehow aware of her approaching difficulties, the little collier turned away from the wave-lashed coast and an attempt was made to gain something of an offing. Great green seas broke across the heavily-laden vessel, and in time water began to make its way below through the accommodation doors. Such were the conditions that on occasion some water even came down her tall funnel, but it was not until she was about 30 miles offshore that she really began to feel the full force of the storm. Throughout the Monday she battled against the ever-rising seas, and to the increased alarm of her crew more and more water found its way on board. At 2.30am on the Tuesday the captain set his six-man crew to bailing, whilst he put his helm down and ran in towards the coast. Water was washing into the bunkers, and as it slowly rose its motion forced up the very stokehold deck plates. Stoking the fires became increasingly difficult, with lumps of coal being passed literally from hand to hand during short spells from bailing.

As the winter morning wore on, the "Fairy" gradually raised the land, and some nine miles off Girdleness made distress signals to a nearby trawler. This was the "Hendrick", a German vessel, whose crew reacted immediately by passing a line and taking the waterlogged collier in tow. This was done at about 10.00am and very slow progress was made towards port, the two vessels eventually being spotted by coastguards manning the Bridge of Don lookout post. A close watch was kept on them through the frequent and heavy snow squalls, but little ground was gained in the heavy seas. The daylight faded early, and by 4.30pm the cortege had reached a point just off the Donmouth. A flare then split the darkness to indicate a need for further assistance, and whilst it was being answered by the watching coastguards, the rescue services swung into action. Both of Aberdeen's life-boats were called out, and the Newburgh crew was put on stand-by at their station on the Ythan estuary. Also alerted were the Bridge of Don and Belhelvie rocket life-saving appliance teams, who quickly took their heavy equipment to the shore.

Aberdeen's No. 2 (Beach) Life-boat, the "Robert and Ellen Robson", under the command of Coxswain George Walker, stood by at the boathouse for some two hours before commencing the road journey to the scene. The No. 1 (Motor) Life-boat, "Emma Constance", was launched immediately, leaving port at 4.38pm with Coxswain Tom Sinclair at the wheel. The harbour entrance was a raging mass of white water, so even the big 61-foot Barnett was tossed about like a cork as she fought her way through the breaking seas. Her windscreen was shattered, luckily without injury to anyone in the cockpit, and a 24" oak beam was split by the sheer force of the waves. George Flett, the Second Coxswain, thought that the vessel's entire casing structure would be torn from her deck by the violence of the motion. Eventually the turmoil on the bar was behind them, and with the sea astern the life-boat ran northwards. Around 5.30pm she came up with the plucky German trawler and her wallowing tow, by this time some two miles off the Donmouth. The "Hendrick" was labouring to keep the collier's head up to the sea, but became increasingly unable to do so as the casualty's weight caused both vessels to wallow heavily in the troughs.

Coxswain Sinclair closed to within hailing distance of the "Fairy", and asked her master if

The collier "Fairy" ashore after her crew had been taken off by the "Emma Constance".

all was well on board. The fury of the storm was such that it was difficult to hear the reply, but Captain Croxford indicated that he would like to hang on as long as possible. Accordingly the life-boat moved clear, and remained in close attendance as the convoy slowly crept shorewards. At this point watchers ashore saw a fourth set of lights heave into view, and then a searchlight began to blink from the newcomer as a message was passed. The new arrival was the Swedish steamer "Montrose", and as she reported damage to her steering gear, the life-boat proceeded towards her. Once the larger vessel was no longer in danger of fouling the tow, the "Emma Constance" left her and returned to the "Fairy's" position. There she found that things had taken a significant turn for the worse as the long-suffering towline had parted under the added strain of encountering broken water.

The trawler's skipper, demonstrating exceptional seamanship skills in the immensely difficult weather conditions, took his vessel round and made a gallant attempt to renew the tow.

The "Emma Constance" enters Macduff after her marathon service to the "Fairy".

This proved impossible, and so the brave little ship, belonging to a nation with whom we were soon to be at war, but whose crew had performed with humanity and considerable courage in the true traditions of the sea, stood clear. It was now up to the life-boat, which, rolling and pitching wildly as she approached, moved towards the casualty. By now the tide had turned and the ebb was carrying the collier northwards, her drift being followed by the LSA teams as they moved their gear towards the Black Dog. Also visible through the squalls were the lights of the "Montrose", out of danger now but standing by to offer any help she could. "Are you ready to come off yet?", called the life-boatmen, but there was no unanimous decision on board the crippled "Fairy". Some of her crew were ready to abandon ship but some were not, and in the event the elements soon resolved their doubts in dramatic fashion.

At about 10.00pm she struck the sand, and with their vessel swept from stem to stern by the seas, her crew at last called for the life-boat to take them off. Cautiously the "Emma Constance" made her approach, but such was the fury of the storm that the life-boat was lifted bodily over the casualty's rail. All on board thought the end had come. but mercifully the next sea came howling across the deck, and washed her clear to try again. Once more she came in, and exhausted though they were all seven of the "Fairy's" crew leapt for the wildly-tossing life-boat, Captain Croxford being the last to leave the stricken vessel. As one crewman made the perilous transfer to the "Emma Constance" he slipped and fell between the two vessels. At no small risk to himself, Life-boatman John Masson reached down and grabbed hold of the seaman and wrestled him aboard the rescue craft.

Thankfully Coxswain Sinclair coaxed his damaged command clear of the casualty and headed seawards towards the waiting "Montrose". Bringing to within hailing distance of the steamer, the Coxswain requested that word might be passed to the North Pier that everyone had been taken off the collier, and were safely on board the life-boat.

Gladly the "Montrose" sent this message — to the beach by lamp, and to Aberdeen by wireless. This was necessary as, despite the requests made after the arduous "Strathebrie" service, the "Emma Constance" still had no wireless fitted. The message was passed on to the North Pier, and then relayed in confirmation to the various shore parties still standing by. The "Robert and Ellen Robson" was turned about and, hauled by her tractor, proceeded back to Aberdeen, reaching the boathouse around midnight. All attention was now focussed on the North Pier; the returning "Emma Constance" should have arrived by 11.30pm, but at 1.00am the next morning, 27 January, there was still no sign of her. A crowd of silent watchers, relatives and crew members returned from the Beach lifeboat, gathered, and many a fearful eye was turned towards the mountainous seas hammering across the harbour entrance. At times these crashed right over the lighthouse on the South Breakwater, and such were the conditions that even the stoutest hearts amongst the onlookers may have begun to fail.

The shocking state of the bar was quite evident to Coxswain Sinclair when he had left port, and even the ''Emma Constance'' had not been damaged during the outward crossing or the actual rescue, it is unlikely he would have attempted to return that night. In the event he felt instinctively that to attempt to enter harbour at Aberdeen would be a recipe for disaster, but without wireless he was totally unable to advise anyone ashore of his intentions. The weather was now too bad for him to re-locate the ''Montrose'', and it was equally impossible for the searchlight to be used to pass even the briefest of messages. He had decided to run for shelter in the Moray Firth, planning to enter one of the ports on its southern coast, but without this knowledge Footdee had to watch and wait, minds fighting not to think the worst.

The ''Emma Constance'' crew after the ''Fairy'' service. Left to right: John Masson, Coxswain Tom Sinclair, Jim Cowper, John Noble, 2nd Coxswain George Flott (at rear), Mechanic Alex Weir.

The "Emma Constance" undergoing repairs in Macduff after the "Fairy" service.

Putting the sea astern once more, the life-boat headed north and once Rattray Head had been rounded to the westward, into the calmer waters of the Moray Firth. In the lee of the land conditions quickly improved, but Macduff was the only port available, and the battered rescue craft entered the harbour at 4.30am on the Wednesday. As soon as the "Emma Constance" came alongside, the crew of the "Fairy" were taken ashore for hot baths and a meal, their first for three days. Word of their safe arrival was flashed to Aberdeen, where it was greeted with considerable relief in Footdee. Loud in praise of their rescuers, the collier's survivors were kitted out with new suits before being sent to Aberdeen on the morning train. George Flett recalls his own trousers as having been torn beyond repair during the service, so he was loaned a pair by the hotel's helpful manager. They turned out to be a few sizes too large, and "a few reefs were taken in" to restore him to respectability. The "Emma Constance" herself had to remain at Macduff for a further two days while temporary repairs were done in Jones' Shipyard, and then she was able to return to her station.

On 6 April, 1937, it was announced that the RNLI's Silver Medal for gallantry had been awarded to Coxswain Sinclair for his part in the rescue of the "Fairy's" crew. Bronze Medals went to the mechanic, Alex Weir, and crew member John Masson, with the Institution's Thanks on Vellum being presented to the other members of the "Emma Constance's" company.

The actual Investiture was held in London's Central Hall, on 9 September, 1937, the medals being presented by HRH the Duke of Kent. In addition to the three medal winners, Life-boatman James Cowper also travelled to the capital to accept the Vellums as the representative of the other crew members. Perhaps the best summing-up of this service is contained in a message sent to its Aberdeen station by the Institution's Headquarters. "The service to "Fairy" carried out in snow, squalls, darkness and rough seas, was a fine example of determination and courage."

Aberdeen life-boatmen amongst the RNLI's 1937 medal winners. From extreme left: Coxswain Tom Sinclair, Alex Weir, John Masson, Jim Cowper.

Thursday, 4 November, 1937, was destined to be a very long day for the crews of the Aberdeen and Newburgh lifeboats. In fact it began at one minute after five that morning, when in response to a telephone message from the Belhelvie coastguards the duty attendant at Aberdeen's North Pier first raised the alarm through Footdee's sleeping squares. Coxswain Tom Sinclair, Second Coxswain George Flett, crew members Alex Weir, Bert Esson, Tom Walker, James Cowper and Alex Sinclair, hurriedly pulled on their clothes and ran through the cold darkness to Pocra Quay, where the reserve life-boat "J and W", lay at her moorings. On this occasion the station's own life-boat, the "Emma Constance", was away from the port undergoing a badly-needed refit, but in accordance with RNLI policy a replacement vessel from the Reserve Fleet had been provided. Quickly the engines were started, mooring lines let go and by about 5.20am the life-boat was rounding the North Breakwater, heading towards Belhelvie.

In foggy conditions the Aberdeen trawler "Delila", of 77 tons, and under the command of Skipper George Slater, had run aground a short time previously on one of several offshore sandbanks, despite the firing of warning flares from the nearby Coastguard lookout post. These were seen too late, and the vessel stranded firmly on the sand some distance offshore. As soon as they saw the trawler's own distress flares the coastguards called out the Belhelvie LSA team, and telephone messages requesting immediate life-boat assistance were passed to the Aberdeen and Newburgh launching authorities. The latter station's craft left her riverside base on her tractor-drawn trailer at 6.00am, and made her way southwards along the sandy shore-line, whilst the Aberdeen life-boat reached the scene some 22 minutes later. Manoeuvring up-tide through the rising sea she anchored, and then veered down on her cable until she lay close to the casualty. As a warning portent of events much later in the day, a heavy surf was already running, so a rope was passed from the trawler to steady the life-boat whilst coxswain and skipper discussed their intentions. The trawlermen elected to remain on board, and planned to refloat their vessel on the rising tide later that morning. At about 7.15am the Newburgh life-boat arrived, having made very good time along the shore, and was launched and rowed out to the "Delila". She also put a line on board, and Coxswain Youngson was told of the intention to wait for the flood tide. He accordingly decided to return to the beach, and to remain there on standby in case he could be of further assistance. In the meantime the "J and W" also moved clear of the trawler and moved into deeper water, often to be lost from view in the ever-increasing sea.

The trawler "Delila" shortly
before she was refloated,
with the "J and W" in
watchful attendance.

The Aberdeen tug "St Machar" arrived around 11.30am, and the "J and W" ran in to transfer a line to the stranded vessel. By this time both the sea and the surf had risen significantly, and the life-boat took a fair battering as she crossed the broken water. The tow was quickly secured, and by noon the tug had the strain. However the "Delila" was still firmly aground amidships, although her bow and stern were both afloat, and it was not long before the line parted. The casualty had been moved some 50 to 60 yards to seaward, and was now stranded on the outermost sandbank, the pounding surf beginning to slew her broadside on. The life-boatmen saw that the trawler's engine was still going astern, so with the sea crashing over them they closed to within hailing distance and shouted for the skipper to go full ahead. A wave signalling his understanding, and with foam boiling under her counter the "Delila's" head slowly began to swing round into the sea. A moment later she slid free of the clinging sand, and with a triumphant blast from her whistle, stood clear of the shore. Escorted by the life-boat she headed southwards, and entered port at 3.15pm. The Newburgh boat's crew recovered their craft, made up their gear, and headed northwards, whilst their Aberdeen colleagues were back on their moorings by 3.45pm.

A very successful service, which lasted almost 10½ hours — a stout ship and the lives of her nine men saved with no small life-boat assistance. However, the day was by no means over, and tragedy was to strike during both stations' next service.

About 9.30pm that same evening the people of Newburgh spilled into the village's streets as the repeated blasts of a ship's siren reverberated above the clamour of the storm. The weather had been deteriorating all that day, and by now a full South-easterly gale was blowing, building up a viciously heavy sea. This was now boiling across the bar at the Ythan's mouth and up the adjacent sandy beaches, but the noise of the siren was alien to the storm. It brought large numbers of people from their homes, many running through the darkened sand dunes to the beach. In their passing they alerted the crew of the Newburgh life-boat and there was a rapid assembly at the boathouse, where equipment was readied for whatever the night might bring.

Those first arriving on the deserted and storm-swept beach could just see the lights of a vessel lying offshore, but the visibility was poor and nothing could be made of its identity. Flames could also be seen on the vessel's forward part: perhaps her crew were burning their bedding, this being one of the traditional signals of a ship in dire distress. Suddenly all the lights went out, the flames as well, and there was only darkness, with the noise of the surf crashing on the shore. The watchers immediately feared the worst; that a huge sea had engulfed the unknown vessel and her crew, and that she had sunk.

The Collieston, Belhelvie, and Bridge of Don LSA teams were called out, the Newburgh life-boat was brought down to the beach, and a message was passed to Captain Wyness at Aberdeen requesting assistance from his station. For the second time that day the North Pier attendant called out the crew, and having been provided with the most up-to-date information available, the "J and W" slipped her moorings about 10.00pm. A very heavy sea was now running on the bar, but she fought her way through it and once more headed northwards on service. The incident's location was believed to be close to that of the earlier service to the "Delila", and once again Coxswain Tom Sinclair was at the wheel. All but one of his crew had been with him that morning, yet they responded just the same, with John Noble taking Alex Sinclair's place.

Whilst the life-boat ran through the night, the LSA teams were engaged in searching the beaches: the Collieston men working southwards towards the Ythan, and those from the Belhelvie, southwards from its mouth. Nothing was found during the course of the first gale-lashed sweep, so the shore parties expanded their search to cover a total of four miles of coast-line. The Newburgh life-boat, still on its carriage, had in the meantime been taken along the beach to the point where the vessel had last been seen. Not long after, the sea began to wash grim evidence of disaster on to the streaming sands; first the Collieston team found two fish boards, both newly-immersed, but without any identifying marks, and then came a find which put an end to any lingering doubts. Again to the north of the river, a life-belt, this quickly followed by a small ship's boat. Both carried the identification "A371", the official registration of the 84-ton Aberdeen trawler "Roslin".

The Aberdeen life-boat had by then reached the position originally given by the Coast-guard, between one and two miles north of their Belhelvie lookout post. It was bitterly cold and flying spray was mixing with the mist to reduce visibility to only a few hundred yeards. There was no sign of any vessel in distress, so Coxswain Sinclair began to work slowly northwards along the edge of the broken water, the "J and W"'s powerful searchlight being used to probe inshore. To the south of the Ythan the Belhelvie LSA men were still doggedly searching through the storm when, incredibly, they heard the thin sound of a human voice calling for help. Just as the LSA team were about to flash a message to the life-boat, whose lights were barely visible through the gloom, it also pinpointed the stranded trawler. By now it was around 2.00am, and the "Roslin" could be seen lying awash some 200 to 300 yards south of the river's mouth. She was a terrible sight as she lay in the surf, almost submerged by now, and swept from end to end by every passing sea. In the glare of their searchlight the life-boat's crew were horrified to see men clinging to the foremast rigging, and it was also noticed that the upper part of the wreck's wheelhouse had disappeared.

Despite the urgency of the situation, conditions were such that it took a long half-hour before Coxswain Sinclair was able to bring the life-boat close enough for a line to be thrown to the survivors in the rigging. No less than six times he ran in, and on each occasion was contemptuously thrown aside by the huge breaking seas. During one such approach the life-boat's forefoot was thrown above the level of the trawler's bulwarks, and then smashed down to cause considerable damage forward. At last a line was grasped by one of the soaked survi-vors, and he immediately attempted to tie it around one of his shipmates who seemed to be in a poor state. This man lost his grip before the line could be secured, and without a sound he dropped heavily on to the deck below. A moment later a huge sea crashed on board, and when it had gone there was no trace of him. Another line was thrown, grasped, and successfully made fast. The man left his frail refuge to leap into the sea, seconds later being dragged on board the life-boat. As he was taken into the cockpit another run was made and the same procedure adopted with the last remaining trawlerman.

Swept in her turn by the surf, but with her weary crew not quite at the end of their tether, the life-boat backed off, turning to make a thorough search of the seething waters until it was evident that there could be no more living survivors. Sadly, for no less than six men had died that winter night, the rescuers turned towards home. The "J and W" arrived off Aberdeen at about 5.00am, and having safely crossed the bar, secured to a quay. The two trawlermen were transferred to a waiting ambulance and a few minutes later were admitted to the recently-opened Royal Infirmary for treatment.

During the return passage the younger survivor, 20-year old George Cowie, of Mansfield Place in Torry, was able to tell his rescuers what had happened on board the stricken vessel. He and his fellow-survivor, Kenneth Cormack, of Elmfield Place, had been asleep in their bunks below, when around 9.30pm they were awakened by the sound of the "Roslin's" siren. Grabbing their clothes and lifejackets they rushed on deck, only to find it being swept by every passing sea. Quickly they ran for the safety of the foremast rigging, and on scrambling clear of the worst of the sea, they found the two engineers already hanging on. The remaining four members of the trawler's eight-man crew — the mate, who was acting as skipper on this trip, the second hand, the cook and the sole fireman — had already sought sanctuary in the wheel-house. On the exposed foremast the second engineer had been the first to succumb to the bitter cold; he lost his grip, fell into the surf and was washed away into the darkness. The three

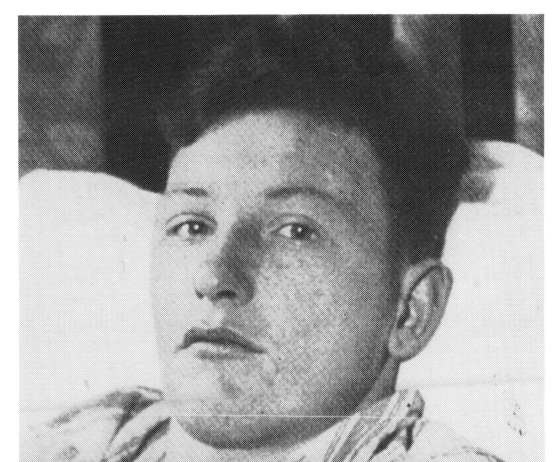

Safe in hospital — George Cowie, one of only two survivors from the trawler 'Roslin".

men still clinging to the foremast rigging could hear, above the roar of the storm, the sound of their four colleagues singing hymns in the wheelhouse. Then a huge sea smashed past, tearing away the wheelhouse's roof, and taking its four occupants to their deaths. Shocked by this the survivors had virtually abandoned hope of rescue when they saw the life-boat, but when Cowie had grabbed the first line and attempted to secure it around the chief engineer, tragedy again struck and the latter fell to the deck.

The "J and W" had been damaged during this mission also, with a piece torn from her stem low down, but the Institution was not long in recognising the Aberdeen crew's heroism. For the second time that year, the RNLI awarded Coxswain Tom Sinclair their Silver Medal for Gallantry, and Bronze Medals were also awarded to Second Coxswain George Flett, and Acting Mechanic Bert Esson. Each of the remaining crew members received the thanks of the Institution, inscribed on vellum.

Captain Wyness, Harbourmaster, and Honorary Secretary (Marine) of the Aberdeen station made the following comment on his Report of Service, "The behaviour of the crew under such conditions, and the almost hopeless position the "Roslin" was in when they arrived in the vicinity was, in my opinion, excellent. I may specially make mention of T Sinclair, the coxswain."

(Authors note: 2nd coxswain George Flett in remembering this service, told the author that the elder survivor, Kenneth Cormack, was the brother in law of Newburgh life-boat coxswain Mr Youngson.)

The trawler "Roslin" ashore off the Ythan mouth.

The War Years

In common with all other British life-boat stations, Aberdeen provided assistance to numerous vessels after the outbreak of war — aircraft, ships and vessels of every kind following attack by the enemy or the elements, for the latter's many hazards were in no way diminished during the period of hostilities. True to the Institution's long-established traditions, this help was freely given to the casualties of every nation, enemy as well as allied, but because of wartime press censorship restrictions and incomplete Service Reports, accurate details of local missions are unfortunately somewhat sparse.

Less than two short weeks after the outbreak of war, the "Emma Constance" was launched during the early hours of 15 September to go to the aid of a reportedly-torpedoed steamer. The "Robert & Ellen Robson" was also put on standby as the casualty's position had been given as "off Carron Point." However, only an hour after leaving port, Coxswain Tom Sinclair was told that the life-boat's services would not be required, and he accordingly returned to the station. Total time on service was two hours ten minutes.

Just three weeks later, during the late evening of 4 October, 1939, the Aberdeen trawler "Stromness" was returning from the fishing grounds, and fighting her way into the teeth of a full South-easterly gale. In the strong wind, heavy seas, and blackout-intensified darkness, difficulty was experienced in making out the harbour entrance, and as she closed the land still further the trawler went aground on a sandbank. Skipper Stanley James immediately went full astern, only to discover that the impact had jammed his vessel's steering gear. The "Stromness" had stranded just off the Beach Ballroom, with the tide now on the ebb, and her bow pointing uselessly towards the Promenade. The casualty's siren was soon blasting out distress signals, and a large crowd quickly gathered to watch the drama unfold.

From the north came the Bridge of Don LSA team, and from the south the trailer-borne surf life-boat "Robert & Ellen Robson". Some considerable difficulty was experienced in moving her down to the shore, but eventually she reached the water's edge, and while she was being manoeuvred upwind of the stranded trawler, the LSA team managed to fire a line across the latter's foremast. The life-boat was launched into the boiling surf, for the site was too far north of the harbour entrance to benefit from its lee, and as she came abreast the "Stromness" her stern touched briefly on the sand. The next sea took advantage of the loss of steerage way, and the hapless life-boat was swiftly swept past the casualty. Two oars were broken, and these difficulties were further compounded by the rocket line fouling both crew and oars. Once clear of the tangle, the life-boatmen quickly resumed their stroke, but their efforts to pull back

The trawler "Stromness" ashore on Aberdeen Beach.

against the crashing seas were without avail and the "Robert & Ellen Robson" beached some 200 yards to the north of the stranded vessel. As this occurred the LSA team fired yet another line, and this time it was secured, with the breeches buoy soon being rigged and the crew of the "Stromness" coming ashore without further incident. The life-boatmen's problems were even then not over as the tractor had broken down during the launching, and it had to be man-hauled out of the surf before the boat could be recovered and taken back to Footdee.

Only a few days later on 10 October, 1939, the "Emma Constance" spent 7½ hours on a fruitless search for the Swedish steamer "Solstad", reported as being short of coal and with steering defects. The Service Report records the weather as "stormy", but despite this the life-boat made a long and thorough search without any sign of the distressed vessel being found. The report also states that the "Emma Constance" had her searchlight and the foot pedal for operating the capstan carried away, and that on returning to her station it was learned that the steamer was already under tow to Leith.

A long-awaited promise to the City of Aberdeen was fulfilled on 29 October, 1939, when the brand-new motor surf life-boat "George and Elizabeth Gow" arrived on station. Almost 50 years previously, in 1890, a Mrs Elizabeth Lovick Gow included in her Will a bequest, "to Mr Duguid Rae Milne, solicitor of 16 Union Terrace, Aberdeen, the sum of Fifteen Hundred Pounds for the purpose of buying and endowing a life-boat to be used at Aberdeen, and to be named the 'George and Elizabeth Gow'.'' Following the payment of death duties the legacy amounted to some £1,350, this sum being placed on long term deposit as no need was then seen for another life-boat. At the time of the station's transfer to the RNLI in 1925 the amount had swelled to no less than £4,000 and by 1938 it had risen to £6,650. At that time it was decided to replace the pulling surf boat ''Robert & Ellen Robson'' with a 35' 6'' Liverpool class vessel, so Mrs. Gow's well matured legacy was accordingly made over to the Institution. No press coverage seems to have greeted the arrival of the new motor life-boat, but the minutes of a Harbour Commissioners' Meeting held during November 1939, record that the craft had arrived on 29th October, and successfully completed all her trials during the following day.

The ''George and Elizabeth Gow'' was classed as a ''non-selfrighting motor sailer''. This

The No.2 Lifeboat ''George & Elizabeth Gow'' at her naming ceremony.

The "George & Elizabeth Gow" at sea (above) and outside her Footdee shed (below).

type had first appeared in 1931, the selfrighting capability having been sacrificed in favour of better initial stability. The hull was divided into six watertight compartments, and 149 air cases were also provided for buoyancy. The single RNLI AE6 petrol engine developed 35 horsepower and drove a shrouded propellor. Her fuel capacity of 48 gallons gave the new life-boat a range of 50 miles at full speed of 7¼ knots. 45 survivors could be packed into her in addition to her crew. A full suit of auxiliary sails were also carried.

Launch and recovery of the
"George & Elizabeth Gow".

The War Years

Some 24 hours after these trials had been carried out the ''Emma Constance'' was once more at sea on another long wartime service. On 31 October 1939, the 4,666 ton Newcastle registered Cairn Line steamer ''Cairnmona'' was torpedoed and sunk off the North East coast, with several local life-boats taking part in the search for survivors. The ''Emma Constance'' spent hours scouring the sea around the position she had been given, but to no avail, and when Coxswain Tom Sinclair reached Peterhead after over nine hours at sea, he learned that the casualty's 31 survivors had already been landed by that port's lifeboat. Three of the steamer's firemen were killed when she was hit — unusually for a local war loss the ''Cairnmona'' was sunk by a submarine rather than an aircraft, and in this case U-13 was responsible.

The ''Emma Constance'' returns to port towing an aircraft dinghy during the war years.

The "Emma Constance" was once again at sea (on a near 20-hour service) during 18 and 19th December, this time searching for survivors from the 203-ton Granton trawler "Trinity NB". She had been bombed and sunk some 80 miles ENE of Aberdeen, and although at least two of her crew were killed, the remainder were picked up by another vessel and taken to the then neutral Norwegian port of Bergen for repatriation.

More Luftwaffe raids took place on 9 January, 1940, with heavy attacks being made against shipping off the Angus and Kincardineshire coasts. The 689-ton Dundee registered coaster "Gowrie" was bombed and sunk some five miles south of Newtonhill, but nearby vessels went in and picked up her 12-man crew. Not so lucky was the Copenhagen-registered steamer "Feddy", which lost her second engineer when she was hit, and the "Ivan Kondrup" from the same port, was set on fire. Both vessels, as neutrals, were marked and lit as required

The Danish steamer "Feddy" enters Aberdeen Harbour after being bombed off the port.

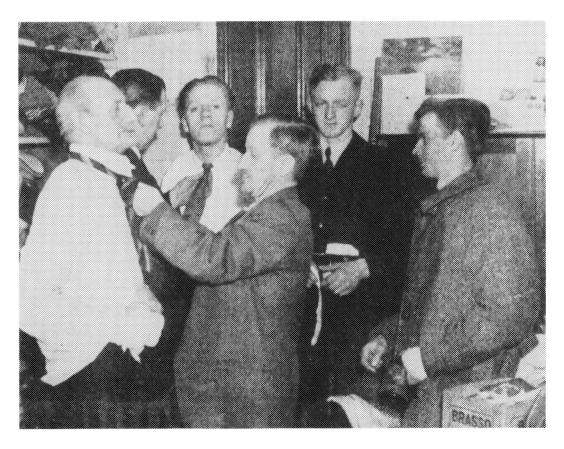

Neutral seamen lost many of their possessions when the ships "Feddy" and "Ivan Kondrup" were bombed, and had to be kitted out in Aberdeen.

by International Law, yet they were bombed and reportedly even machine-gunned as their crews took to the boats. Service details of these incidents are unfortunately incomplete, but it seems that the "Emma Constance" spent 7 hours 20 minutes at sea, picking up two men from the "Feddy" and four from the "Ivan Kondrup". She spent a further 9 ½ hours on service the next day, standing by as the still-smouldering "Feddy" was towed into Aberdeen.

On two more occasions during that fateful spring and summer of 1940 (3 March and 16 July) Aberdeen's life-boats were launched to go to the assistance of unknown vessels as the Luftwaffe tightened its grip on local sealanes, but nothing was found on either service. A more positive result was recorded following the attack on the 20 October, 1940, on the 4,876-ton steamer "Conakrian". The vessel, registered in Freetown, Sierra Leone, was torpedoed some nine miles SE of Girdleness, and the "Emma Constance" was launched at 9.50pm. She reached the position around 10.10pm, and whilst carrying out a search, one of the crew saw something in the darkness. The searchlight was switched on and in its beam the horrified life-boatmen saw the conning tower of a submarine. The light was doused in an instant, the helm put hard over and rapidly increasing to full power the "Emma Constance" left the scene with considerable rapidity.

Two miles further on she came upon a Royal Navy destroyer which signalled that she had taken 29 "Conakrian" survivors on board. As an apparant afterthought she then advised that there was a British submarine in the area, and it is presumed that this was greeted with more than passing relief by the life-boatmen.

Shortly after this drama, the casualty itself was sighted, and the "Emma Constance" stood by to await the arrival of a tug which was reported to be in its way from Peterhead. In the black-out the latter had to be directed to the scene by the life-boat, and it was not until around 3.00am on 21 October that the crippled merchantman was taken in tow. By this time the tide had carried the casualty some four miles to the northward of the port, so with the "Emma Constance" as guide, the little convoy reached Aberdeen Bay where it was anchored at about 4.00am. Total time recorded on this service was 7 hours 40 minutes, and the next day saw a further 1½ hours at sea following a request by the local naval authorities for the life-boat to take off two RN personnel. This was because bad weather prevented the use of other boats, but the "Conakrian" story was by no means over as, early on the morning of 23 October, she developed a heavy list. At 3.30am, with a moderate easterly gale blowing, at the request of the Naval Officer in Charge of the port the "Emma Constance" put to sea, taking off 23 men from the anchored steamer, and returning to her station at 4.42am. This service seems not to have been recorded locally, but it is known that it was quickly and skillfully carried out despite the autumn darkness and heavy breaking seas running into the Bay.

Despite continuing Luftwaffe attacks on local convoys, with numerous Allied vessels being sunk or damaged, the winter of 1940/41 saw no calls for the port's life-boats, and it was not until 3 April that the "Emma Constance" next put to sea on service. This followed the sinking, south of Stonehaven, of the tiny coaster "Greenawn" and the near-missing of another, the 250-ton Methil-registered "Cairnie". A bomb caused considerable damage to the stern of the little ship as it exploded close by, but she staggered on through a rising South-easterly gale. Only at the entrance to Aberdeen harbour was it realised that the steering had been crippled by the force of the explosion, and the vessel was now out of control. Her crew were by now exhausted following their brush with the enemy and force of the storm, so distress signals were made at 8.30pm. Less than 20 minutes later, the "Emma Constance", with George Flett at the wheel, was fighting her way through the heavy seas rolling into the navigation channel, and soon approached the wallowing coaster. Running alongside, and sustaining damage to her fendering forward on the starboard side, the life-boatmen swiftly took the casualty's seven-man crew on board. The "Emma Constance" was back at her station by 10.00pm, but the unfortunate "Cairnie" went ashore on the beach, it not having been possible to do anything more for her in the atrocious conditions of that night.

Some ten weeks later, on 13 June, 1941, the "Emma Constance" was launched on service to yet another bombed merchant vessel. This was the 5,796 London-registered "Dalemoor", which had been hit and set on fire some seven miles South-east of Girdleness. Leaving port at 1.30am, the life-boat was quickly on the scene, and found the steamer burning fiercely. The weather was good, and several other vessels were standing by. One of them, reported variously as a corvette or a mine-sweeper, signalled that she had 39 survivors on board, and requested that a search be carried out in case there were any more. This was done, with the "Emma Constance" spending the dawning day sweeping around the blazing derelict until a tug arrived. Shortly before 4.00am the life-boat assisted with the passing of a tow from the tug to the three-man salvage party previously put on board the "Dalemoor" by the latter. Once this had been done it was seen that the flames were spreading, and at the request of the tug the "Emma Constance" went alongside the casualty to take off the three navymen. Coxswain Sinclair returned them to their vessel and went on to resume the search for survivors, eventually returning to station after a service lasting more than six hours.

The next life-boat related incident of any moment seems to have taken place during the evening of 15 March, 1942, following the stranding of the newly-built corvette "HMS Hyderabad" on the North Breakwater. An escort vessel of the "Flower" class, "HMS Hyderabad" had been constructed by Messrs A Hall at their Footdee yard, and had presumably been on trials at the time of her grounding. At 6.40pm, with Coxswain Tom Sinclair at the wheel, the "Emma Constance" was launched, to find a southerly breeze blowing across a heavy ground swell in the navigation channel. At 8.25pm the steam tug "Bruno" arrived, and whilst attempting to put a line on board the casualty, herself went ashore on the west side of the old South Breakwater. At this point the "Emma Constance" was released from standing by the corvette, and asked to go to the assistance of the tug. The "Bruno" was rolling and pounding in the surf, but it was not long before a line was passed and efforts begun to refloat

The corvette HMS Hyderabad.

her. Thirty minutes later these succeeded, but with a vengeance. As she came free, the "Bruno" gathered sternway quickly, striking the life-boat heavily aft and damaging the latter's port quarter. It was then discovered that the tug had lost her rudder whilst ashore, so forgiving the unprovoked assault, the life-boat towed her back to her berth. In the interim, "HMS Hyderabad", had been able to work clear of the North Pier, so the "Emma Constance" was able to return to station after a "front door" service lasting some 4½ hours.

No reports have been located for services on 14 April, 1942, to the Aberdeen trawler "Bon Accord" nor on 2 April, 1943, to "unknown vessels", but there are details of an incident involving the Faroese auxiliary motor schooner "Else" on 7 April, 1943. At about 10.20am she had been seen in apparent difficulties off the South Breakwater, and with a strong northerly wind gusting up to gale force it was decided to provide immediate life-boat assistance. The "Emma Constance" was quickly launched, and on reaching the scene found that a naval vessel had already taken the schooner in tow. A further line was passed by the life-boat to counter the effects of the heavy sea at the harbour mouth, but it parted under the strain. Shortly after the other line also broke, but the casualty was by then able to proceed under her own power, and all three vessels safely entered port at 11.30am.

During 1943 the No. 2 (Surf) Life-boat "George & Elizabeth Gow" joined the Royal Air Force, probably the only RNLI vessel to serve abroad with the armed services. Being of the motor beach-launched type she was ideal for the rough seas found around the Azores. These islands were at that time an important staging post for aircraft flying between North America and United Kingdom, and it is presumed that the life-boat was taken to provide rescue cover in case of accident. Whilst "called up", the "George & Elizabeth Gow"'s place was taken by the veteran pulling life-boat "Robert & Ellen Robson".

Royal Air Force Marine Craft section personnel manned the "George & Elizabeth Gow" whilst she was based in the Azores, and although details of her foreign service are lacking, she is reported to have rescued two fishermen in trouble. On another occasion, the life-boat (still

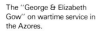
The "George & Elizabeth Gow" on wartime service in the Azores.

apparently in RNLI colours) towed a Walrus amphibious biplane from rough waters to a calmer area where it could safely take off. Following her "demobilisation" the "George & Elizabeth Gow" returned to Aberdeen in 1947, and the "Robert & Ellen Robson" departed for Whitby. There she remained in service until as late as 1957, moving on as the only pulling life-boat preserved in a seagoing condition to that port's Life-boat Museum.

The report on a service to the St Ives-registered "Trevorian" on 29 November, 1943, is unfortunately incomplete, but there is much more information on that to the Dutch steamer "Kielehaven" almost 11 months later. At 6.15am on 23 October, 1944, the local RN authorities requested the "Emma Constance" to launch and proceed to a vessel some ten miles east of the port. As it was almost calm, with a moderate Southerly wind, the life-boat soon covered this distance, and at 7.30am she came up with the merchantman — fully laden — but with no-one on board. A nearby RN trawler signalled that the steamer's 49-man crew had abandoned her (no reason for this is known), and were now on board another vessel in the area, the US-registered "Henry Austin". With the life-boatmen understandably somewhat bemused by all this, the "Emma Constance" went alongside the liberty ship, and took on board no less than 40 men. All were from the "Keilehaven", and at the request of her Master, he and several others were put back on board their vessel. The remainder were taken to Aberdeen, whilst the casualty was eventually brought into port.

The last two services recorded during the war in Europe took place within three days of one another, and both involved foreign fishing vessels. Late on the evening of 10 April, 1945, the Faroese fishing smack "Albert Victor" drifted on to the Beach whilst attempting to check her compasses. She had earlier arrived off the port with a full cargo of fish for British markets, and as she was then ordered to Hull for discharge, an Aberdeen skipper was put on board to assist with the coastal navigation. A tug was quickly on hand with a line, but was unable to tow her off. With the tide on the ebb it was decided to call out the life-boat to remove the casualty's crew for the night. The "Emma Constance" was soon on the scene, and after making several attempts to run through the heavy surf, went alongside and took off a total of nine men. Damage was sustained to the life-boat's starboard guardrails, and the passage skipper's foot was slightly hurt as he boarded the "Emma Constance". Total time on service was some 3 ½ hours, and the "Albert Victor" was refloated a day or so later.

Early on the morning of 13 April, 1945, word was received that another vessel was aground on the Beach, and not far from the stranded Faroese smack. This was the Ijmuiden-registered

The Faroese smack "Albert
Victor" ashore on Aberdeen
Beach.

58

trawler "Maria", and although there was little danger in the good weather then prevailing, it was decided to launch the life-boat. As the tide rose the Dutch trawler skipper asked the "Emma Constance" to run out two kedge anchors, and when this had been done it was only necessary to await high water. The "Maria" refloated herself without any difficulty, and with the life-boat in close attendance she entered the harbour for survey. Service time was around six hours, and a little less than a month later European hostilities ended.

The Post War Forties

Late on the afternoon of 22 May, 1945, the large RN motor torpedo boat MTB 2007 was in-bound to Aberdeen, one of a fair number of naval craft still using the port, despite the end only a fortnight previously of the war in Europe. Although many of these fast craft had used harbour facilities during hostilities, this particular MTB had a somewhat unique background in that she had served in both the Royal and Merchant Navies. Originally built for Turkey by Messrs Camper & Nicholson, she was taken over for RN use, and because of her large size — 117 feet overall length with endurance to match — was converted into a fast cargo vessel and renamed ''Gay Corsair''. A number of her class were similarly treated and with Merchant Service crews, ran on blockade-breaking missions between UK East coast ports and Sweden. Operating under conditions of the most extreme secrecy they carried large quantities of vital war materials such as precision machine tools, with at least one such mission setting out from Aberdeen.

A moderate North-easterly wind was kicking up a somewhat confused sea across a deep ground swell as the MTB entered the navigation channel — one of the most dangerous conditions which can occur in the harbour entrance. For some reason, and probably com-pounded by the following sea, the MTB swung to port, losing steering control, and within a few moments she was hard aground on the rocks some 150 yards to the east of the old South Breakwater. Immediate efforts were made to tow her off, with the reserve life-boat ''John Russell'' being launched at 5.50pm to assist with the passing of lines and running anchors out into deeper water. It was soon apparent that these efforts would be unsuccessful as the MTB's frail hull was becoming more and more damaged with the pounding it was taking, and it was eventually decided to take off the crew. One navyman had in fact already been injured and was brought ashore by the Torry LSA Brigade. The heavy breaking swell had made the early part of the operation difficult as well as hazardous.

Some time after 9.30pm, and in the gathering darkness, the life-boat ran in once more through the heavy seas, which were by now sweeping right over the casualty. No less than three approaches were in the end required before the remaining twenty RN personnel were taken off, and on the last run the ''John Russell'' suffered damage from striking against the hull of the by now partly submerged warship. The rescued navymen were taken the short distance to Footdee, where they were given into the care of the RN authorities, and it was not long before the life-boat was back on her station. Over on the Torry shore the wreck began to break up, and after only a few days she seemed to have gone almost totally to pieces. However her shattered forepart lay on the rocks for many years thereafter as a reminder of one of the local

H.M. MTB 2007 wrecked in
the Navigation Channel.

life-boat's more obvious services and also of the port's inherent perils. The ''John Russell'' had later to undergo local repairs for her hull damage.

RNLB ''John Russell''

Following the drama of the MTB 2007 mission, the remainder of 1945 was somewhat uneventful. Aberdeen's life-boats carried out five more services, totalling 17 hours 49 minutes, in response to calls to search for ditched aircraft, a tow for disabled minesweeper, and the provision of escort for yawls in difficulty. For the first 1946 service no Report has been found, but from press accounts, it was a thoroughly unpleasant experience. The Grimsby trawler "Spurs", on her first fishing trip after being derequisitioned by the Admiralty, was attempting to enter the port to land a sick man during the evening of Sunday, 20 January, 1946. In the darkness and heavy seas she stranded on the North Pier, and then, with her propellor damaged she drifted helplessly across the navigation channel to ground on the south shore. The tug "St Machar" and the "Emma Constance" were both called out, but the former also went aground, and some time during the consequent confusion the casualty refloated, only to strand again in the same area. Whilst standing by, the "Emma Constance" first fouled both her propellors on lines from the trawler, her mast was snapped off by another rope, and finally she was thrown against the "Spurs" and damaged. Eventually the Torry LSA Brigade took off most of the trawler's crew, the remainder climbing down the bow at low water and wading ashore. The tug seems to have been refloated without serious difficulty, and press reports indicate that the "Emma Constance" had to go to Buckie for repairs, her relief taking a pounding during her passage to the port as the bad weather lingered on for some days thereafter. She even had at one point to put into Fraserburgh to repair storm-damaged steering gear.

Members of Torry LSA team pass lines to the trawler "Spurs"

The Post War Forties

As Coxswain Tom Sinclair proudly watched his Boy Scout stepson collecting his award at the Corporation Swimming Bath ceremony, he was handed a message, and within a few seconds had taken abrupt leave of the gathering of scouts and parents and was running through the February darkness. He had just been told of a ship ashore at Belhelvie, and with the night of 5 February, 1948, being a stormy one with strong SSE winds, there was no time to linger. The first report of the incident came in at around 8.00pm, and the "Emma Constance" was soon on her way on what was to prove to be the longest service of her distinguised career — 78 hours, 10 minutes.

The casualty was the Aberdeen trawler "Northman" inbound from the Faroe grounds, and uncertain of her exact position in the poor visibility and heavy seas. All of a sudden the coast

The trawler "Northman" ashore off Belhelvie.

near Belhelvie came into view just ahead, and almost simultaneously the trawler went ashore on the wave-lashed sand. With no steam the casualty's 12-man crew had to light nets on the foredeck as a signal of distress, and this was soon seen from ashore. The Belhelvie LSA team was quickly on the scene, and it was not long before they had their rocket apparatus rigged to fire lines out to the stranded "Northman". At 9.55pm, the "Emma Constance" arrived, and some two hours later, whilst attempting to work alongside in the thick winter darkness, she too went ashore.

The LSA team's efforts to rig a breeches buoy eventually met with success, and the 12 trawlermen were safely brought ashore as the Newburgh life-boat made its way southward on its carriage. True to long-standing local tradition, the local people had been quickly on the scene to help with the heavy work of hauling on the breeches buoy gear, one Balmedie woman telling the Coastguard, "Ye canna' stand aroond wi' yer haunds in yer pooches at a time like

"George and Elizabeth Gow" attempts to tow "Emma Constance", aground during the "Northman" service.

this!'' The seven-man crew of the ''Emma Constance'' despite being wet through, and constantly swept by bitterly-cold breaking seas, spent the next few hours trying to refloat their craft, but without success. They tried again on the afternoon high tide, again with no sign of movement, and at 4.00pm they were taken off. A taxi took them back home for food, a brief rest, and a change into dry clothing, but only five hours later they returned to try yet again. Every high water for the next three bitter days saw the crew, assisted by the No 2 life-boat ''George and Elizabeth Gow'', working to refloat their stranded vessel, but it was not until 1.25am on 9 February, with the help of the tug ''St Fotin'' that she slid free of the sands. That she was virtually unscathed by her experience and able to return to port under her own power was a glowing tribute to her builders and also to the strength of the 22-year old vessel.

Aground — ''Northman'' and ''Emma Constance'' share a sandbank.

The next year, 1949, saw the end of an era in Aberdeen life-boat history. After almost a quarter of a century as the No.1 life-boat's coxswain, and earlier experience with the port's pre-RNLI organisation, Coxswain Tom Sinclair decided to call it a day and retire. Awarded the Institution's Bronze Medal in 1935 for his gallantry during the "George Stroud" mission, and no less than two Silver Medals for the 1937 services to the "Roslin" and "Fairy", Coxswain Sinclair was described by Aberdeen's Lord Provost as "A man who has some magnificent deeds to his credit". Speaking at the annual Life-boat Ball in the Beach Ballroom, Lord Provost Fraser went on, "You have had a very meritorious life, and Aberdeen should be proud of you." The big Coxswain, whose reputation for having nerves of steel is still local legend, played a major part in the saving of some 200 lives from a wide range of distress situations during his life-boat career. His last service, on 15 January, 1949, was to the Grimsby trawler "Welbeck", which had gone aground just north of the harbour entrance. The weather at the time was perfect, a far cry from conditions during many other services of Tom Sinclair's experience, but the "Emma Constance" was handled with the same degree of skill as she ran towing lines to the local tug "Danny". From call-out to escorting the refloated trawler to port occupied almost 2½ hours, and then Coxswain Sinclair, the first holder of the local RNLI post, returned to his home in Cotton Street, and passes out of our story.

Coxswain Tom Sinclair receiving his retirement testimonial from Lord Provost Duncan Fraser.

The Post War Forties

His replacement as Coxswain was George Flett, another pre-RNLI veteran. As a member of the old pulling life-boat's crew during the October, 1923, service to the trawler "Imperial Prince" he had been washed overboard, but undeterred by this experience had gone to sea in the Merchant Navy. He then returned to Aberdeen, and was appointed a Harbour Pilot, additionally becoming a prominent member of the life-boat crew.

RNLB "Emma Constance" bows out after 25 years of service.

A New Lifeboat R.N.L.B. `Hilton Briggs´

The "Emma Constance" was also about to follow her coxswain into retirement after an equally honourable career at the port. In August, 1951, her replacement, the 52 foot Barnett class lifeboat "RNLB Hilton Briggs" was completed in a Cowes, Isle of Wight shipyard, and following RNLI acceptance trials she sailed northwards to her new station. Unusually some of her passage was on fresh water for she spent three days at Nottingham as a major Festival of Britain attraction, being open to the public and attracting considerable attention. Her building, at a cost of around £25,000, had been funded by a legacy left by a Mrs. Briggs of Southport, and the vessel was named in memory of the donor's late husband. Somewhat smaller than her predecessor, "Hilton Briggs" was powered by twin 50 horse power diesel engines which gave

The "Hilton Briggs" at Gorleston during her delivery voyage.

A New Life-boat R.N.L.B. "Hilton Briggs"

her a top speed of 9 knots and a range at that speed of 180 miles. A simple cockpit amidships afforded a minimal shelter for her coxswain, and a similar, smaller cockpit aft provided for the crew's "comfort". (After her departure in 1959, an enclosed wheelhouse was fitted). The Barnett was designed to carry 100 survivors plus her crew in rough weather.

Her arrival in Aberdeen on 30th August saw a crowd of some 400 people, including the city's Lord Provost, in eager attendance. She was met by the "Emma Constance", and the two vessels entered port in company, a brief ceremony being held to mark her taking up station duty. The formal naming was not due to be held until the next year, and equally there was no haste in the departure of the "Emma Constance". Stripped of her engines and most of her fittings, she lay forlorn until eventually being towed to Sandbank, near Dunoon on the Clyde, where she remained for five more years. (The hulk was eventually purchased by two Frenchmen who converted her to a pleasure craft, spending considerable sums on her refit. They were unable to take her away however, for some financial reasons, and I believe she still lies in Sandbank. *Author*).

The "Hilton Briggs" arrives in Aberdeen.

70

The "Hilton Briggs" puts to sea "in a bit of a blow".

The Fifties

The "Hilton Briggs" had to wait until January, 1952 for her service debut, and in the interim the next local life-boat mission was carried out by the "George & Elizabeth Gow" and a commandeered salmon coble. Once again the River Dee was the culprit as it rose in spate, fuelled by torrential rain and gale-force winds, with the Aberdeen area suffering various levels of flooding as the evening of 5 November, 1951 wore on. Some 20 minutes after midnight on 6 November, Captain Posgate, the Harbourmaster and Life-boat Honorary Secretary, was contacted by the police. They requested assistance in rescuing two people from a caravan encampment at Maryculter, which had been cut off by the floodwaters. As the water had risen to a depth of some eight feet it was decided to use the surf life-boat "George & Elizabeth Gow", Retracing the route of the "Robert & Ellen Robson" on her January, 1937 service to Waterside Farm, the tractor and laden trailer made their slow way along the South Deeside Road, whilst Coxswain George Walker and Captain Posgate went on ahead to assess the situation. Gazing through the rainswept darkness they decided that the life-boat could be launched without it running into the river's mainstream, the speed of which they estimated to be between 15 and 20 knots.

The "George & Elizabeth Gow" being launched for the Mill Inn service.

The journey to the Mill Inn took two hours 20 minutes, and shortly after 3.30am the life-boat was launched into the swirling flood. Shortly after leaving the bank floating debris fouled the propellor, and the life-boatmen had to act quickly to return to the launching site and moor up to consider the matter further. At this point it was noted that the flood seemed to have reached a peak so it was decided to await daybreak before trying again. As the dawn came, it was seen that the water was receding somewhat, and that the current was not nearly so strong. This made it possible to use a small boat, and word was accordingly passed for the requisitioning of a Harbour Commissioners' salmon coble. It arrived on the back of a lorry at about 9.00am, and was immediately put to work. As it was rowed across the flooded fields one of its crew stood forward with an axe, hacking a way through any fences and gates which intervened.

All in all the press-ganged "life-boat" made no less than seven trips through the floods, and found a total of 29 people in the cut-off caravan encampment. As the coble went backwards and forwards the waters continued to drop, and the life-boatmen's last mission was

The "George & Elizabeth Gow" during the Mill Inn service.

The Fifties

carried out on foot! Two of the crew waded out to a farmhouse hard by the caravan site, and when they returned they were carrying 80-year-old Mr A. Stewart, who was totally blind, and his 73-year old wife. It had taken the rescuers quite some time to persuade the old couple to leave their home, and they only agreed when their son, Mr Oliver Stewart, and their Polish farm labourer promised to stay to tend the livestock.

By 2.00pm the rescue operation was complete, and the "George & Elizabeth Gow" her propellor cleared of the obstruction (few RNLI vessels can have been prevented from carrying out their missions by agricultural flotsam!), was put back on her trailer. The long return journey back to Aberdeen began, and continued without incident until the tractor threw a track at the Bridge of Dee. This was at 4.30pm, in the middle of the evening traffic peak, and the consequent police reaction is not recorded. They did however produce a car to race down to Footdee, pick up a spare, and return with it to the scene of the breakdown. By 7.00pm the surf life-boat was safely housed in its shed and ready for its next (more conventional) service.

The "George & Elizabeth Gow" beached after the Mill Inn service.

The ''Hilton Briggs'' was launched on service no less than three times between her arrival on station during September, 1951, and her formal naming ceremony on 2 October, 1952. One of these involved a search for a Royal Air Force Vampire jet which crashed some 20 miles Southeast of Girdleness on 18 August, 1952. This was a long service lasting almost 14 hours, but no trace of the aircraft's two-man crew was ever found.

The day of the new life-boat's dedication was cold and blustery, but this did not deter a crowd of several hundred people from gathering on the banks of the Dee to watch the ceremony. Lord Provost Graham presided, and the new vessel was named by the Lady Provost.

Dressed overall, the No.2 Life-boat attends ''Hilton Briggs'' naming ceremony.

The "Hilton Briggs" at her naming ceremony and taking the guests to sea (below).

The RNLI's District Inspector, Lieut E D Stogdon, said that the experience gained from over a hundred years of life-saving around the coasts of the British Isles had gone into the building of the "Hilton Briggs". However, without her crew of splendid seamen she could not do her work. After the ceremonial events the principal guests were treated to trips down the navigation channel in the new life-boat.

When it is angry the sea can be very beautiful — sinister, menacing, and dangerous — but beautiful just the same. Over the centuries artists have covered yards, if not miles, of canvas and paper to capture the sea in its many moods, particularly those showing it in violent turmoil. People come to the shore to watch the huge seas smashing against rocks and cliffs, throwing clouds of spray high into the air to be whipped away by the fury of the storm. Perhaps it was this fascination which caused a Mr Masson to look up from his work in the local village of Muchalls on the late afternoon of 26 October, 1953. The whole fury of a South-easterly gale is thrown aginst these little villages clinging to the clifftops southwards from Aberdeen, and their storm views can often be spectacular indeed. For this reason perhaps it was fortunate for four Stonehaven men that Mr Masson had paused from his work to look out at the storm, for as he did so the red glare of a distress flare rose above the cliffs.

The Stonehaven yawl "Trustful III" had left her home port at 6.00am that morning on a regular fishing trip, and some four hours later, her crew were shooting their gear about three miles off Muchalls. A piece of deck matting blew over the side, and as Skipper David Andrew turned his vessel round to retrieve it, one of the warps fouled the yawl's propellor. For two hours the fishermen struggled in the rising wind and sea to clear the obstruction, but without success. Having eventually recovered their gear, they hoisted the small mizzen sail, hoping that the flood tide would drive them up to the Bay, where they could expect to be seen from the shore. However the wind was stronger than the tide that autumn day, and the yawl was driven in towards Muchalls and the waiting rocks. The skipper had the anchor dropped about a mile from the wave-lashed shore, the little vessel coming to an uneasy mooring in the heavy seas. Around 4.15pm her crew fired a distress flare.

As soon as he saw the red glare, Mr Masson wasted no time, and within a few minutes was on the telephone to the Coastguard at Gregness. By 4.30pm the "Hilton Briggs" was on her way to the rescue, commanded by Coxswain George Flett, fighting her way southwards through heavy seas with almost every wave bringing water on board. The life-boat provided little shelter for her crew — a matter which was to become a major problem over the course of the next few years. There was merely a cockpit amidships to provide some protection for the helmsman, and a smaller one aft. As a result the crew were drenched even before they rounded Girdleness, and as the gale rose to Force 8/9 — almost 45 knots of wind — speed was drastically reduced. Although the distance to Muchalls is only some ten miles it took no less than an hour and 50 minutes to reach the village, and it was 6.15pm before the crippled yawl was in sight. Coxswain Flett made his first approach on the windward side, but before the towline could be passed it became obvious that the "Hilton Briggs" would be in danger of fouling the yawl's straining anchor rope. As a result the life-boat was taken round the casualty's stern, and brought up towards the leeward side. Two attempts had to be made before the heaving line, thrown against the wind, could be caught by the tired and cold fishermen. Eventually the life-boat's tow-rope was passed and made fast, and shortly after 7pm Coxswain Flett was able to call for power on his engines. (In those days the two mechanics operated throttles in response to the helmsman's verbal instructions). With the lee shore not far distant no chances could be taken, so the life-boat crept ahead with extreme care to avoid parting the tow. As the "Hilton Briggs" and her burden altered course to the northward (it was patently impossible to make for Stonehaven in those conditions) the ever-rising seas made for laborious progress, with the yawl either threatening to crash into the life-boat's stern or to fall astern and part the rope. Time passed without incident, but about a mile south of Girdleness the tow did part under the strain, and the life-boatmen hauled it in as Coxswain Flett swung round into the storm to come up on the yawl's lee side between the rocks and casualty.

By now it was 8.20pm and darkness had fallen, with the "Hilton Briggs" approaching to

RNLB "Hilton Briggs"
entering harbour.

reconnect the tow as the two vessels drifted to within 200 yards of the boiling seas beating on the Gregness rocks. On this occasion the first cast of the heaving line would have to be on target for there would be no chance for the second. In the event the thin cord flew true, to be seized and the heavier rope hauled in. Once he was satisfied that the tow had been secured on board the wildly-pitching yawl, Coxswain Flett was faced with the arduous task of clawing off the lee shore still so close under his stern. Great difficulty was experienced with this, the need to "nurse" the line being paramount, but eventually the life-boat could alter course and run in towards Aberdeen. The service report contains no mention of the return across the harbour bar, but given the wind's direction and strength, it cannot have been an easy or pleasant crossing for the crews of either the "Hilton Briggs" or the "Trustful III".

Once safely in port the yawl was towed to the Fishmarket, and helping hands soon had her berthed alongside. The life-boat returned to her station, and the service report ends with laconic statement "Ready for service 22.15". Perhaps more relevant were the comments of the Honorary Secretary, Captain Lindsay Traill, who was full of praise when he wrote, "The sea-manship displayed by the Coxswain and crew of the 'Hilton Briggs' under the worst of weather conditions, increased by the backwash from the proximity to the shore, could not have been surpassed."

One of the fourteen officially-recognised signals for a vessel in distress is the continuous sounding of the ship's siren or foghorn. It was such a signal that George Flett, Aberdeen life-boat's Coxswain, heard at his Bridge of Don home on the foggy night of 20 October, 1955. Immediately recognising the signal for what it was, he telephoned the harbour's hailing station at the North Pier, and then headed towards the life-boat's Footdee moorings. It was around 9.35pm, and George Flett's report was soon confirmed by another message, this time from a Mr James Taylor, of Newburgh, who was parking his car near the Broad Hill. He had also heard the siren, and peering out to seaward through the rolling banks of fog, saw a distress flare rising out of the murk.

The source of these signals was the 88-ton Aberdeen trawler "Sturdee", returning to her home port after eight days on the fishing grounds. Skippered by William Wilson of Macduff, she had a complement of 11 men, and whilst nosing cautiously through the foggy darkness, stranded about a quarter of a mile to the north of the Beach Ballroom. As she lay on the sands, constantly swept by the breaking seas and heavy surf, the crews of Aberdeen's two life-boats were called out at 9.45pm. The "George & Elizabeth Gow" was rolled out of her shed on her tractor-drawn carriage, and made her ponderous way along the Beach, whilst the "Hilton Briggs" crossed the harbour bar at 10.15pm.

Although the wind was blowing at only 15-20 knots from the south there was a heavy breaking sea, and to effect the rescue the life-boat came alongside the casualty's lee side — in fact between the "Sturdee" and the shore. To keep her stern to the sea, the life-boatmen deployed the drogue, or sea anchor — a conical contrivance made of heavy canvas, bound to wooden hoops and wire strengtheners. During the run in to the stranded trawler only the one sea caught the "Hilton Briggs". Curling across the life-boat's stern it crashed on board, flooding the tiny after cockpit where crew member George Walker hung on to a stanchion as well as the drogue line. "One hand for the ship, and one for yourself", runs the old seaman's watchword — and the less reverent may on occasion continue, "and if one ain't enough for yourself, then to hell with the ship!"

However "Spud" Walker knew that if he did let the drogue line go, the chances were that the next curling sea would throw the stern round, with the near-inevitability of the life-boat capsizing and throwing her crew into the surf. Instinctively he held on to both the stanchion and the drogue, and the sea drained away leaving him soaked but unhurt, although his glasses had been swept from his face. More importantly the "Hilton Briggs" was still on course for the casualty, and as the life-boat came alongside, the drogue was recovered and a line thrown to the fishermen.

In the meantime the Coastguards had not been idle, for whilst the life-boats made their separate ways to the scene, the Bridge of Don LSA team had been mustered and were soon on the beach with their equipment. Searchlights quickly illuminated the scene, and a large crowd gathered while the fog cleared somewhat as if to assist the recue services. A rocket line was

The crew of the "Hilton Briggs" come ashore after the "Sturdee" service.

fired, and flew across the trawler to lodge in her foremast rigging, the Coastguards' intention being to bring the Sturdee's crew ashore by breeches buoy. However, with the "Hilton Briggs" coming alongside, this operation was temporarily suspended.

By now it was shortly after 10.30pm, and held by her veering line, the life-boat ranged wildly alongside the casualty. Each time she approached the knot of fishermen one or two more jumped on board, but a total of five or six runs were necessary before all were safe. Skipper Wilson was the last to leave his ship, and then Coxswain Flett was faced with the very real problem of working clear to seaward. The coxswain was, however, quite equal to his task, for holding on to the rocket line forward, he juggled the life-boat's stern clear of the casualty with the engines. Judging his moment, he ordered the rocket line to be cut, and the "Hilton Briggs" slipped round the trawler's bows and headed for the harbour entrance.

The eleven fishermen were landed into the care of the Seamen's Mission at 11.10pm, and the "Hilton Briggs" returned to her moorings. Elsewhere in Footdee the big double doors closed on the "George & Elizabeth Gow", and along the Beach the Coastguards packed up their equipment. The crowds soon drifted away to their firesides, perhaps with a wee dram to dispel the chill of the damp October night, and alone and foresaken the "Sturdee" turned slowly over onto her port side. Eventually she became a total loss, although much of her gear and more valuable equipment was recovered during the following days.

For his skill and courage that night Coxswain George Flett received the RNLI's Thanks inscribed on Vellum, his fourth award in 22 years of service.

The trawler "Sturdee" aground off the Beach Ballroom.

The Fifties

The station's busiest year seems so far to have been 1956, with no less than 11 calls being recorded for the lifeboat's services. It was also the year that the growing dislike for the port's choice of No. 1 Life-boat came to a head. The "Hilton Briggs", as has previously been mentioned, had no enclosed accommodation for her complement, only an open cockpit amidships for the Coxswain and mechanics at the engine controls, and a similarly-exposed compartment aft for the remainder of the crew. In the eventual opinion of the Aberdeen men she was thus ill-equipped for the long services so often called for along the NE Scottish coast, and several 1956 missions more than adequately seem to have proved the validity of their thinking. On 30 January, the "Hilton Briggs" was launched to escort two fishing vessels into port — the previous day the trawlers "Junella" and "York City" had rescued the crew of the German coaster "Gertrud", of Leer, following that vessel's capsize in heavy weather some 140 miles off Peterhead. The casualty's nine-man crew had been thrown into the water, but had managed to scramble on to the upturned keel of their stricken vessel. Demonstrating consummate seamanship the trawlers had been able to run alongside and rescue the Germans from their precarious

"Hilton Briggs", showing the open forward cockpit.

82

refuge. Shortly after, the "Gertrud" sank, and the rescuers made haste through the Southerly gale to land the survivors at Aberdeen. Given the sea state it was decided to request the life-boat to launch and provide expert advice on local conditions, as well as standing-by to escort them into port. As a result, the "Hilton Briggs" slipped her moorings at 1.50am, and moved to take up station in the navigation channel. Coxswain Flett contacted the "Junella" and "York City" by radio and informed their skippers of the heavy breaking swell on the bar, as well as of the five-knot spate running down the river. When he was sure the trawlermen were fully aware of the situation and the best way to handle the approach to the port, the coxswain "talked" both vessels over the bar before putting pilots on board. The life-boat was back on her moorings by 3.30am, and the survivors were taken to the Fishermen's Mission for a hot meal.

Just ten days later the "Hilton Briggs" was again at sea. The 7,000-ton American cargo vessel "Mormacoak", on passage to New York with a cargo including paper, had signalled that her Chief Officer had been seriously injured when several of the half-ton rolls had become dislodged during a hold inspection. The ship accordingly headed for Aberdeen to seek urgent medical attention, and also to have the cargo restowed before resuming her voyage. The "Mormacoak" arrived off Girdleness just after 7.00pm on 9 February, 1956, right on low water. This meant that the deep-draught cargo vessel would be unable to enter port for some hours, and as the injured man was miraculously still alive after being pinned to the deck by no less than 16 rolls of paper, the life-boat was launched at 7.05pm with Dr. John Leiper, the Port Medical Officer, on board. A little later the "Hilton Briggs" reached the freighter, and "Dr John", as he was affectionately called by the life-boatmen, climbed up the pilot ladder and was immediately taken to the sick bay. It took him only a few minutes to decide that the Chief Officer, suffering from head and face injuries as well as a fractured femur, could not be transferred to the life-boat, and would have to remain where he was until his ship docked. He accordingly released the "Hilton Briggs", which was back on station by 9.05pm, and an ambulance was waiting for the injured officer when the "Mormacoak" docked shortly after midnight.

The next life-boat service took place on Sunday, 18 March, when at 8.50pm the duty operator at Stonehaven Radio intercepted a wireless message through the Cullercoats station. This was from the Russian steamer "Krymov" to her agents, Messrs John Cook, and requested assistance because the vessel had stranded. As the position given was very close to Aberdeen the local coastguard was immediately informed, and the report was swiftly confirmed by a sighting of a ship ashore some two miles north of the Donmouth. It was not long before the

The Fifties

The Coastguard LSA team
fires a rocket line to the
stranded Russian steamer
''Krymov''.

84

No contact — the stranded Russian steamer "Krymov".

Bridge of Don LSA Team was on its way, and the "Hilton Briggs" was soon clearing the harbour. The night was overcast, with moderate visibility and a strong SE breeze, and in the steamer's position a heavy sea was running. This made an approach from seawards difficult, and to add to the life-boatmen's problems, they were met with a total lack of communication from the Russian crew. The offers of help, made by both radio and loudhailer, were utterly ignored, and the same response was made to signals from the shore party, who went as far as firing a rocket line over the casualty. For some three hours the "Hilton Briggs" remained in the immediate area, but in direct contravention of one of the basic traditions of the sea, there was no contact from the stranded vessel, and eventually it was decided to return the life-boat to her station.

Early on 29 March, 1956, the trawler "Rennyhill" was returning to Aberdeen from the fishing grounds when she encountered thick fog off the port. Whilst feeling her way towards the harbour entrance she took the ground on the seaward side of the South Breakwater, and sent out a distress signal. The "Hilton Briggs" slipped her moorings at 3.30am, and cautiously (radar was many years away for either the life-boat or the port) proceeded to the scene, "homing-in" on the blasts from the casualty's siren. In the meantime the coastguard had alerted the Torry LSA team, and it was not long before they had their equipment in place on the shore. After considerable difficulty the life-boat's tow-line was passed on board, and the "Rennyhill" was pulled clear with her rudder and propellor both damaged by the rocks. As a result Coxswain Flett did not find it easy to tow the crippled trawler, and it was not until almost 8.20am that she and her eight-man crew were safely alongside.

Almost five months were to elapse before the next service, and on this occasion it was accompanied by an element of farce. Five young RN artificers from Rosyth had decided to make something of a busman's holiday of their three-week summer leave by purchasing an ex-ships life-boat from a scrapyard and sailing it to Findhorn. Just south of Montrose they landed and set about preparing a meal, only to find that port's life-boat drawing alongside. They had been mistaken for survivors from the German lugger "Adolf", which had sunk a few days previously! Undeterred by this incident the five intrepid mariners continued northwards — straight into more drama! By midnight on 16 August the coastguard at Aberdeen were becoming concerned over the whereabouts of the navymen, and at 12.30am the duty officer called Captain Traill, the Hon Secretary, to request a search. The "Hilton Briggs" had left the station the day before for refit, and her replacement, the "JJKSW" was put to near-immediate use. Not being entirely familiar with the reserve vessel, the crew had difficulty in starting one of the engines and it was not until the life-boat was in the navigation channel that the second was running.

In the event the navymen were found within 15 minutes, lying becalmed some two miles off Girdleness without a care in the world, blissfully unaware of the commotion their non-arrival had caused ashore. However they did accept the offer of a tow, and were safely moored in Aberdeen harbour by 1.45am.

On 3 November, 1956, the freshly-refitted "Hilton Briggs" spent four hours searching Aberdeen Bay and down the coast as far as Stonehaven following a report of an upturned dinghy, but without success. Investigations ashore revealed no boats missing, and the report, made from a telephone call box, was put down as a hoax.

The crew were assembled twice more during the early winter — on 6 and 7 November, but on neither occasion was the life-boat required to put to sea. The first incident followed the forced landing of a Dyce airport-based RAF Vampire near Murcar, and the second the stranding of the fishing vessel "Stephens". The latter was attended by the Peterhead life-boat, and the crew was taken off by the Collieston LSA team.

The following day, 8 November, saw the "Hilton Briggs" at sea once more, on a nine-hour service in dirty weather which reinforced the life-boatmen's dislike of their open-cockpit vessel. This was to the Oslo-registered vessel "Solskin" under the command of Captain Hendrik Hugdahl, bound from Krageroe in East Norway to Aberdeen with a cargo of 1,100 tons of wood pulp. At 10.00am that morning the freighter was about 60 miles east of Tod Head, rolling heavily in the big seas generated by the strong SE wind. Just after her captain had reported her ETA to his agents a sea carried away one of the hatch covers, and the cold North Sea came flooding in to be greedily absorbed by the wood pulp cargo. Swiftly she began to list to port, and when Captain Hugdahl sent the distress message, his ship was heeling over to about 22 degrees. Putting the heavy sea on her quarter the casualty headed in towards the coast; a nearby Belgian trawler, whose name is unfortunately not recorded, coming crashing to her aid, and remaining in company. Donning their life-jackets, the Norwegians began pumping, encouraged by the fact that every mile they covered brought them nearer to the coast and

The Fifties

safety. Ashore, the rescue services were by now fully alerted, and at 12.44pm Coxswain Flett took the "Hilton Briggs" to sea, pounding into the teeth of the gale and dodging the torrents of water which almost continually deluged himself and his crew. After over three hours of this misery the life-boat reached the "Solskin", some 35 miles from the port, and took over escort from the gallant Belgian. Soaked and frozen the life-boat crew's ordeal continued as they followed the listing Norwegian shorewards, being encouraged by news that the casualty's pumps were holding the flooding. Finally, at 9.00pm the two vessels entered port, with the "Solskin" mooring at Commercial Quay, where her 16-man crew went for a hot meal. As for the life-boatmen: despite their fatigue they had to fuel as soon as they moored, and the debris of the trip had to be cleared up. Only then was "The Submarine", as the "Hilton Briggs" was now called in Footdee, ready for service, and her crew in their turn could stand down.

Only 17 days later, on 26 November, 1956, another somewhat similar call came, again to a Norwegian, and as far as the Aberdeen crew was concerned it was the last straw, with all their smouldering dislike of the conditions on board the "Hilton Briggs" flaring to the surface. On this occasion the wind was blowing at Force 9 from the NW, and it took no less than six and a quarter hours to reach the casualty. The Trondheim-registered freighter "Strindheim", with a timber cargo had been battling through heavy seas when her crew discovered six feet of water in the hold, and this soon caused a ten degree list. The "Hilton Briggs" was launched at 5.45pm in response to the Norwegian's distress call, and it was midnight before she came up with the

Relief Lifeboat "JJKSW".

casualty, by now some 33 miles off the port. In close company the freighter and her escort battled through the teeth of the gale, reaching Aberdeen Bay and relative safety just after 6.00am. With life-boatman George Walker at the wheel the battered "Hilton Briggs" ran in alongside the "Strindheim", and Coxswain Flett climbed on board to pilot her into port. The service is recorded as having ended at 7.10am on 27 November, and the crew's long-muted rumblings were about to erupt.

As the soaked, exhausted, and frozen life-boatmen came ashore it was obvious to the waiting press that the crew had been through a nightmare trip, and the newsmen soon sensed that all was not well. The headline in the following day's "Press & Journal" proclaimed "LIFEBOATMEN COMPLAIN — HILTON BRIGGS NOT SUITABLE FOR THIS COAST — CLAIM". The article went on to say that the impression gained by those who met the life-boat on their return had been that unless something was done to improve the protection of the crew in stormy weather, there was likely to be difficulty in finding volunteers to man the "Hilton Briggs". After the "Strindheim" service the "Journal" discussed details of the life-boat's problems — the open cockpits which provided little shelter so that the crew was always wet through — the difficulty of steering her in any following sea because her propellors were so near the stern. Comparisons were naturally drawn between the "Hilton Briggs" and the "Emma Constance", the latter vessel having heated accommodation under cover, and facilities for making hot drinks, being obviously the Aberdeen crew's favourite. The hard-hitting article concluded with a comment from the RNLI's Scottish Inspector, who stated that then-current life-boats the size of the "Hilton Briggs" did not have enclosed wheelhouses.

Whilst the local crew were unhappy and dissatisfied with conditions on board the "Hilton Briggs", her seaworthiness caused them no concern, and just two days later they responded to another call — thankfully the last for 1956. The Grimsby trawler "Lombard", owned by the Lindsay Steam Fishing Company and with a crew of 13, was on her way to the grounds in company with another fishing vessel after the Christmas break. The date was 29 December, and the winter night was an unusually thick one, with very poor visibility in the gentle breeze. The "Lombard" was navigating by radar, keeping what her crew thought was a little less than a mile offshore. In fact her equipment was picking up echoes from the high ground inshore of the coast, and she was actually considerably closer to the land than was appreciated at the time. Soon she was ashore some two miles south of Newburgh, and Skipper Fred Warman, fearing that his ship was about to capsize in the heavy broken surf, sent out distress signals. These

The trawler "Lombard" aground near Newburgh.

were received and passed on to the Hon Secretaries of the Aberdeen, Newburgh, and Peterhead life-boat stations. The "Hilton Briggs" launched at 7.45pm, to head northwards in the bitter cold. No accurate position was available for the casualty so it was not until around 10.00pm before the searching life-boat, her navigation lights extinguished to counteract the glare of the fog, reached the scene of the stranding. The trawler lay very close in with her stern to the heavy surf, so Coxswain Flett had the drogue streamed to keep the life-boat straight as he ran in through the breaking seas. So close were they to the beach that more than one life-boatman thought he was going to have to walk home that night — and so it very nearly proved! The drogue line "hummed" with the strain as the "Hilton Briggs" crept inshore, and then, to seaward, a curling white shadow climbed high astern out of the fog. Some six to eight feet it rose above the life-boat's rails, then crashed down with tremendous force — a "dumper". The "Hilton Briggs" staggered under its weight, tons of water flooding the open steering position, and rushing through the partially open "kitchen" door of the radio cabin to leave the wireless and direction-finding sets a steaming, useless mess. Perhaps it was as well that the cabin was flooded as otherwise the sea could have washed George Flett out of the cockpit. As it was the life-boat had lost its communications, the searchlight bracket had been fractured, and worst of all, two of the crew had been injured: Bowman John Allen and 2nd Mechanic John Martin had been thrown heavily against the casing.

Tripping the drogue, the life-boat turned about and retired to lick her wounds. The crew hailed the ''Lombard'' through the fog and asked the position of the companion vessel. ''About ¾ of a mile off'', they were told, so the Hilton Briggs'' made her way clear of the surf and asked the trawler to pass a message ashore requesting an ambulance to be available on her return to harbour. In the meantime the Newburgh life-boat was able to launch off the beach, and coming alongside the ''Lombard'', Coxswain Donald Robb was told that the crew intended to remain on board, with the aim of refloating their stranded vessel. The ''Hilton Briggs'' returned to Aberdeen at 1.10am, and John Allen was taken to hospital for treatment to his arm — his ''holding on'' arm, which had been almost wrenched from its socket by the force of the ''dumper''. The Grimsby men were unable to refloat their vessel, and after almost 24 hours they were able to walk ashore at low water. So far up the beach had the ''Lombard'' been driven that it was some six months before she could be freed from the sands, and then it was only for a brief passage to a breaker's yard.

With a tug at hand, the trawler ''Lombard'' awaits salvage.

As if to compensate for the large number of services in 1956, the following year saw Aberdeen's life-boatmen summoned on only three occasions. However, only one of these merits inclusion in this history – the services to the small Danish coaster "Amos" on Christmas Day and Boxing Day, 1957.

The 490-ton "Amos" was on passage to Leith with a cargo of coke chips, and at 7.40pm on Christmas evening she was some 65 miles ESE of Aberdeen, battling into a heavy sea brought up by a near-gale force SW wind. Hans Michelsen, her 51-year old steward, had been taken ill with terrible abdominal pain so severe that morphine was required to ease his agony. The coaster's master, acting on advice from the Danish authorities, sent out a radio call for medical assistance, and this was passed on to Aberdeen Coastguard. In turn they alerted the Port Medical Officer, Dr John Leiper, and he was on board the "Hilton Briggs" when she sailed shortly after 9.00pm. In the interim the "Amos" had altered course to make for Aberdeen, the intention being that the doctor would be transferred when the two vessels met some time the following morning.

The life-boatmen had been enjoying Christmas Day with their families – Assistant Mechanic George Walker had been watching television with his girlfriend, another was eating a dinner of roast duck (which he later 'lost' during the ensuing service). For John Allan Jnr it was his first life-boat service – his father, also John Allan, had been 'in the boat' for some 30 years, but on that stormy Christmas night he was suffering from 'flu, and in no fit state to go to sea. Realising that the "Hilton Briggs" would probably be short-handed, 19-year old John pulled on his seaboots, and ran for the boat.

At 4.09 the next morning the life-boat rendezvoused with the Dane in a very confused and heavy sea. The "Amos" hove-to, and George Flett ran in alongside, passing head and stern lines to hold the "Hilton Briggs" in position. The coaster's crew lowered a ladder for 'Dr John', but after two unsuccessful attempts to grab hold of it in the violent motion, the 53-year old doctor realised he was not going to get on board that way. Opening his medical bag, he filled his pockets with the items he thought he would need, then waiting his chance he leapt, accompanied by George Walker, for the coaster's waist. Safely on board, the doctor was taken to Michelsen's cabin, where after a brief examination, he administered more morphine. With the aid of the Danes, he and George Walker put the sedated steward into a stretcher, prior to his transfer to the life-boat. By this time it was so rough that Coxswain Flett thought his vessel was going to be smashed – the drogue fairlead was shattered, 18 feet of fendering on the starboard side was torn off, as were the adjacent lifelines. Life-boatman John Murray was thrown violently against a stanchion and injured his side, but finally the stretcher was safely on board the "Hilton Briggs". The "Amos" altered course to the southward to resume her passage to Leith, and the life-boat made for Aberdeen. Taking account of the condition of his patient, George Flett decided to run into the lee of the coast and then head north in the calmer water inshore. The doctor or one of the life-boatmen stayed with Michelsen at all times during the long return trip, but the sick man remained only semi-conscious throughout.

With the sea on her bow the "Hilton Briggs" could only make some six knots, so it was not until 5.25pm on Boxing Day that she entered port, to be met at Matthews Quay by an ambulance. After well over 20 hours at sea in atrocious weather Dr Leiper and the seven life-boatmen were absolutely exhausted, but the boat was refuelled and back on her moorings by 7.00pm, and the crew could pick up the lost threads of their Christmas celebrations. Long before, the sick steward had been taken to hospital where a rupture was diagnosed as the cause of his illness.

Crew of the "Hilton Briggs" come ashore after the 20 hour service to the "Amos".

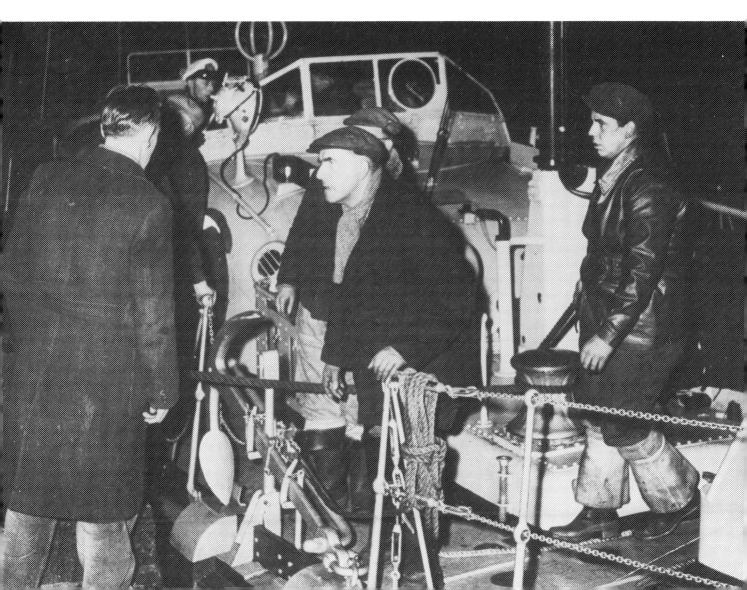

R.N.L.B. `RAMSAY DYCE

The RNLI had not disregarded the comments of the Aberdeen crew and with a new life-boat fitted with an enclosed wheelhouse already on order, the "Hilton Briggs" carried out her last two local services during 1958. Although detailed information is not now available, the Branch Committee had held a meeting to discuss a possible replacement, and to this the crew were invited as well as the Scottish Divisional Inspector of Life-boats, Lt. David Stogdon. The inspector had with him a model of the "Hilton Briggs", on which he pointed out the several features and equipment which made her an outstanding example of her class. The crew in their turn were not convinced, no doubt remembering their experiences during the long and exhausting services to the "Solskin", "Strindheim" and more recently, the "Amos". To reinforce their argument they too had a model with them, hidden beneath the table on the knees of Coxswain George Flett. This was a replica of the well-loved "Emma Constance", and it seems that the crew made it abundantly clear that they considered her a far more suitable vessel for use on the NE Scottish coast than the open "Hilton Briggs". A lady committee member, whose identity unfortunately remains unknown, is reported to have summed up the entire problem and its solution at the end of the meeting, by stating, "We have heard these gentlemen of the crew saying that they want a wheelhouse. They are the people who go to sea in the boat, so if that is what they want, then that is what they should have, and we should get if for them."

In the meantime the work of the station continued. The Granton trawler "Luffness" coming up from the south to land an injured seaman fell victim to the ledge on the North Pier on the morning of 21 January, 1958. The "Hilton Briggs" was launched within five minutes of the call under the command of 2nd Coxswain John Murray and was quickly on the scene. However, the pilot boat and the tug "Danny" had been alerted earlier and were able to take off the trawler's crew prior to the life-boat's arrival. In the reduced visibility caused by persistant snow showers the "Hilton Briggs" was partially successful in her efforts to run moorings between the casualty and the pier. This was done in a reasonable sea state, but was still not without its dangers as the life-boat received moderate damage to her stern.

The last service carried out by the "Hilton Briggs" before the arrival of the new vessel was to the tanker "Steersman" of London, which grounded in thick fog near the Black Dog on 8 May, 1958. The life-boat stood by for two hours prior to being released, but the stranded tanker's crew remained on board to discharge their cargo and assist with salvage efforts.

The Dee was up to its tricks once again during 1958, and as an inevitable result the Mill Inn

94

caravan site was under water. At 2.20am on 29 July the Hon Secretary received a telephone call from the police to request the life-boat assistance as the floodwaters at Maryculter were still rising and there were fears for the safety of the encampment's residents. The use of the "George & Elizabeth Gow" was vetoed, following the 1951 service to the same location and the consequent fouling of the propellor with debris. Instead the Harbour Commissioners provided one of their salmon cobles, and a mixed crew of Footdee men and fishermen were mustered, including life-boatmen George Walker and Bill Cowper. The Fire Brigade supplied a lorry, and not to be outdone, George Flett produced an inflatable dinghy. Just 25 minutes after Captain Traill, the Hon Secretary, had been alerted the party left Footdee by road, and by 3.10am they had reached the Mill Inn.

For just over three hours the sturdy coble and the tiny inflatable plied backwards and forwards between the "shore" and the caravans in the driving rain and darkness, a total of 14 people being brought to safety by the two craft. Not all of these were rescued by the boats — seeing an old lady in one of the vans, and being unable to come any closer whilst afloat, George Walker climbed onto a drystane dyke and began walking along it towards her. According to his close friend and fellow life-boatman Bill Cowper, George called out, "Hang on, missus, I'm coming to get you" — and promptly disappeared. All that could be seen was his "bunnet" on the swirling flood, then he surfaced and was recovered by his mates. Once he had explained the circumstances of his untimely submergence it was several minutes before the crew could recover sufficiently from their mirth to rescue the patient old lady. George had gamely walked along the just-awash dyke, not realising that there was an open gate between it and the caravan, and had walked straight into the gap!

The operation was over by 6.30am and after taking leave of the rescued caravanners, the lorry party returned to Footdee with the coble, inflatable, and 14 tired seamen — tired but pleased with the success of the past night's work.

The day the Aberdeen crew had been waiting for — perhaps at times even praying for — came on 25 September, 1958, with the arrival of the port's third RNLI life-boat, the 52-foot "Ramsay-Dyce" of the well-tried Barnett class. She had sailed from her builder's yard at Cowes on the Isle of Wight during the previous week, and spent 24 hours at Whitby on public display before resuming her delivery voyage. On arrival she was met by a civil party, including Lord Provost Stephen, who welcomed her to Aberdeen. The new vessel was of course fitted with the enclosed wheelhouse the crew had wanted, and this was provided with moveable, all-

R.N.L.B. "Ramsay – Dyce"

The brand-new "Ramsay Dyce" on arrival, with the "Hilton Briggs" alongside.

round windows for maximum visibility. Powered by twin Gardner diesels, each of 72HP, the "Ramsay-Dyce" had a top speed of nine knots and a range of 180 nautical miles. Even in rough weather, she had a capacity of some 100 survivors. As a result, Aberdeen's life-boatmen now had the craft they had been asking for, and as with her two predecessors, they did not have long to wait before the opportunity to test her in earnest arose.

Two fruitless searches marked the advent of 1959, the first on 18 January was in response to two reported sightings of red flares off the Bridge of Don, and the second, on 25 March, was to search in dense fog for the trawler "Cadorna". This vessel was reported to be broken down some three miles NE of the harbour entrance, and although not found by the life-boat despite a six hour 40 minutes' search, was located and towed in by the tug "Danny". On 27 July, 1959, the relief life-boat "James McPhee", on station in the brief absence of the "Ramsay-Dyce", launched in thick fog to go to the assistance of the Dutch fish carrier "Huiberdina Gysbertha".

96

Crew disembark from
"Ramsay Dyce" after a
fruitless search.

She had stranded some three miles north of the port, and with little sea running was able to refloat herself, proceeding under her own power to meet the life-boat. At this point the casualty's master indicated that he wanted to enter harbour and with the visibility being nil, Coxswain Flett went alongside and passed his towline. During the manoeuvre the coxswain had a nasty and personal lesson in the perils of hydrostatics as the proximity of the two vessels resulted in the wheel taking charge and smashing down on his hands and fingers. Once the Dutchman had been safely berthed, George Flett was taken to hospital where an X-ray revealed that nothing was broken, but the heavy bruising was evident for some while.

The "Ramsay Dyce"'s official naming ceremony was held upriver on 1 August, 1959, a special pontoon having been provided for the occasion. The vessel's cost had been defrayed from a legacy provided by a Mr William Ramsay of Dyce, and his niece, a Mrs Evelyn Wellington of Stroud, Gloucestershire, carried out the actual christening. The President of the Aberdeen Committee, Lord Provost Stephen, accepted the new life-boat on behalf of the

R.N.L.B. "Ramsay – Dyce"

Branch, and the proceedings ended with the dignitaries going for the by-now customary trip up-river.

The "Ramsay Dyce" lies
upriver for her formal
naming ceremony.

At 11.15pm on 27 October, 1959, the trawler "David Ogilvie" broker her moorings in a
force 8 NNE gale and drifted off into the harbour. Owned by the North Star Steam Fishing
Company of Aberdeen, the vessel had been moored in the river, and her unauthorised movement into the tidal basin alerted the pilot cutter and the tug "Danny", both of whom
unsuccessfully tried to put lines on board. The "David Ogilvie" came to rest, hard aground, on
the south side of the channel. It was assumed at that time that no-one was aboard. Two pilots
who were attempting to pass towlines saw no signs of life, and with the commotion and the
pounding of the casualty on the bottom, it might have been expected that had anyone been on
board, they would have been both visible and vocal! At 12.25am on 28 October immediate
attempts to refloat the trawler were temporarily suspended, and it was decided to make a fresh
start at daybreak. However, at about 4.00am the police, who had been attempting without
success to trace the casualty's watchman, contacted the Hon Secretary and requested that
the life-boat be called out to make a search of the stranded vessel. The "Ramsay Dyce" left her
Pocra Quay moorings at 4.20am, and ten minutes later ran through the heavy breaking swell to

R.N.L.B. "Ramsay – Dyce"

lie alongside the "David Ogilvie". Two life-boatmen jumped on board and in the laconic words of the service report, "discovered watchman sound asleep on top of cylinder heads in engine room." He was wakened, taken on board the life-boat, and returned ashore. The "Ramsay Dyce" was back on her moorings by 5.30am.

The gale had abated but little later that morning when the life-boat returned to the trawler. This followed a decision that as the latter was a danger to navigation, and as the weather might cause her to break up and block the port for a considerable time, she would have to be refloated as quickly as possible. At that time there were no local salvage companies and also no vessels capable of manoeuvring safely in the heavy breaking seas, so the life-boat was used to put five men, including two of the trawler's engineers, on board. The engineers started the big trawl winch and the "Ramsay Dyce" ran a warp across to the North Pier. The winch took up the slack, but the "David Ogilvie" stayed where she was and the wire parted under the strain. Again the life-boat moved in, and another warp was run across the navigation channel. With the flood tide this effort was eventually successful, and at 8.45am the trawler pulled herself clear. The "Danny" took her in tow, and with the life-boat's assistance, berthed her in the Torry Dock.

The trawler "David Ogilvie".

The Sixties and the Inshore Lifeboat

The October, 1959, service to the trawler "David Ogilvie" was in effect Coxswain George Flett's last rescue. Apart from two "Assembly only" calls around the turn of the year, he was only to put to sea 'in anger' once more, and that mission was cancelled before the "Ramsay Dyce" cleared the pierheads. This was on 14 May, 1960, when the Pilot Cutter, inbound from a ship in the Bay went aground on the seaward side of the South Breakwater. The sole occupant swam some 30 yards to the shore, and when located by the Torry LSA Team, then hot on their way to the scene, was already walking home! Coxswain Flett's long (37-year) career in Aberdeen's life-boats was drawing to a close — since his first pre-RNLI service (in 1923 to the trawler "Imperial Prince", when he was washed out of the pulling boat), he had been decorated no less than four times by the Institution. Coxswain now for 11 years he had decided at age 63 to call it a day. He set the date of his retirement for June, 1960, but unfortunately his withdrawal from the Service he had served so well was not to be without difficulty. The near-simultaneous retirement of Second Coxswain John Murray and Bowman John Allan (the two men next in seniority to the Coxswain) meant that the Branch Committee would have to begin literally from scratch to find a suitably-qualified man to step straight into George Flett's shoes, and also that the retiring crew members would have to stay on until the new man "had the weight".

The Committee soon found their new Coxswain — and in a most unlikely place: Leo Clegg DSC was Lecturer-in-Charge of the Sculpture Department of Gray's School of Art in Schoolhill. A yachtsman and former MGB commander with an excellent war record (his DSC came in recognition of the part he played during the raid on St Nazaire), he accepted the post with pleasure, and "signed on" initially as Second Coxswain to understudy George Flett, who had agreed to defer his departure until the September. In his turn John Allan volunteered to remain until the end of the year to assist the handover. By the time of George Flett's departure Leo Clegg had settled in well — he soon gained the crew's confidence, and as he was only 40 years of age, looked set to remain for some considerable time. However, during the following December a storm blew up to upset the Aberdeen station's new-found equilibrium. "Life-boat Storm at 'Quit' Order to Cox" proclaimed the "Press & Journal" headline on 5 December, 1960, and the front-page article went on to state that the new Coxswain's employers had required him to resign before the end of March next. No reason was given for the decision, and no comment could be obtained from either Leo Clegg or local RNLI officials. The life-boat crew on the other hand — both past and present — were reported to be both outspoken and highly

Coxswain Leo Clegg DSC.

aggrieved. The Coxswain, however, declined to resign, and continued to fulfill his duties, and in February, 1961, his employers extended their deadline until the end of the year. Then, on 30 December the "Press & Journal" gleefully announced a further extension, this time until the end of 1962.

In June, 1962, the 35' 6" Beach Life-boat "George and Elizabeth Gow" (Aberdeen No. 2), was withdrawn from local service. Although the RNLI had provided the Aberdeen station with two life-boats on its 1925 take-over, the No. 1 vessel had carried out the vast majority of services. It would in fact appear that the No. 2 craft was only launched "in anger" on a total of nine occasions between 1925 and 1962. Seven of these services were carried out by the "Robert & Ellen Robson", and only two by the "George & Elizabeth Gow". Admittedly the latter had been absent on several wartime years on RAF service, but her replacement — again the former — was not used at all during her stand-in time. Then, as now, always concerned with the husbanding of their resources the Institution must increasingly have felt that there was no real need for a second Aberdeen life-boat, and early in 1962 it was accordingly suggested that the "George & Elizabeth Gow" be withdrawn. This was agreed by the local committee, and on April 23 it was announced that this element of the Aberdeen organisation was to terminate.

The closing down of the Torry and N Pier LSA units was also announced at the same time.

(The subsequent career of this vessel was not further pursued in the compilation of this history, but the author did note on the Lowestoft Life-boat Station's Service Board a mission to the "RNLB George and Elizabeth Gow", broken down off that port in 1962.)

For some years after the RNLI's departure, the Beach life-boat shed lay empty, and after a spell in the hands of the Royal Naval Auxiliary Service it was demolished to make way for works involving the southern end of the Promenade.

Coxswain Clegg was not at all happy as he with his crew clustering around him, all fully accoutred for a long service, stared in something approaching disbelief at the insistent young woman confronting them. Outside it was snowing gently, the flakes curiously muffling the deep rumble of the life-boat's twin diesels. The girl spoke again, "Dr Leiper is on holiday, Dr Ross is not available, and I am his locum. The ship out there needs a doctor, and here I am!" Shaking their collective heads, the crew assisted Dr Myrtle Farquharson into a spare set of protective clothing, adjusted a lifejacket to fit her smaller frame, and then took her on board. The crew were not lulled into a false sense of security by the calm waters of the harbour and undisturbed snowfall. They knew they had a long trip ahead of them that 14 November, 1962, well clear of the sheltering Aberdeenshire coast, and that they were going to take a pasting from the Northwesterly gale then blowing. As the "Ramsay Dyce" cleared the harbour and set an East-northeasterly course, the ever-growing seas on her port quarter set up a sickening, corkscrewing motion, and many an anxious glance was directed at the brave young doctor on this, her first trip to sea.

The Sixties, and The Inshore Life-boat

Eighty miles from the port the Danish fishing vessel "Poulann" pointed her bluff bows shoreward and made her best speed against the gale to meet the oncoming life-boat. The reason for the mission lay in his tiny cabin — the skipper had lost three fingers severed in an accident some hours previously. By 10.30pm the life-boatmen, expecting to sight the "Poulann" were at their stations all around the deck, searching for her lights, but without success. Dr Farquharson was not at all well by this time but insisted that when the time came she would be able to do her job. The life-boatmen in their turn mentally doffed their caps to her fortitude, and the search continued. Despite use of the searchlight, parachute flares and the radio direction-finding equipment, the "Ramsay Dyce" still failed to sight the Dane, and at 15 minutes past midnight Stonehaven radio called with a new position.

This put the "Poulann" some ten miles astern (inshore) of the life-boat, so the Coxswain put his vessel about and gave chase. However, he was unable to overtake, and the fishing vessel reached Aberdeen at 7.00am, her injured skipper being immediately taken ashore for treatment. The "Ramsay Dyce" berthed an hour later, and Dr Myrtle Farquharson stepped thankfully ashore at the end of her first sea trip, accompanied by the admiration of the life-boat's crew.

Aberdeen life-boatmen of
the 1960's. Coxswain Clegg
at extreme right.

From the "Poulann" service until the end of 1965 the Aberdeen life-boat had a fairly quiet time. True there were 18 services, totalling some 72¼ hours at sea, but in the main these were, as one crewman put it, "run of the mill stuff", with 29 persons being assisted during this period. On 2 February, 1966, however, another real test of life-boat and crew took place, this involving the Grimsby-registered trawler "Ross Fortune".

For Skipper Pat McCarthy in the year-old futuristic-looking fishing vessel it had already been a nightmare voyage, for on 26 January the propellor had been fouled by the trawl, and his 140' long command had been left helpless. Taken in tow by another Grimsby vessel, the "Ross Leopard", McCarthy had hoped that divers in Orkney might be able to clear the obstruction, but his hopes were in vain as locally-available equipment was inadequate for the task. Once again the tow was resumed, the two vessels making their way towards Aberdeen. The little convoy arrived in the Bay on the blustery afternoon of 2 February, 1966, and was met by the harbour tugs "Sea Griffon" and "Sea Trojan". Far from being over at this point, Skipper McCarthy's nightmare was only intensifying, for as the tugs manoeuvred to take over the tow from the "Ross Leopard", the line parted and the casualty went adrift in the rough seas just off the Donmouth. As his ship drifted helplessly shorewards McCarthy ordered the anchor dropped – at this point he estimated that there were just three or four feet of water under his keel, and that he was only 400 yards from the beach. As the stricken trawler was pounded by the rough breaking seas he feared that she would take the ground and turn over, and he knew that if that happened all would be lost.

The Hon Secretary, Captain Lindsay Traill, received the request for life-boat assistance at about 3.20pm, and soon afterwards the "Ramsay Dyce" rounded the North Pier, making all possible speed for the scene. As she did so the tableau unfolded to the crew; the trawler amongst the white water, close in under the shore, and the two tugs standing by as close as they dared. As they pounded through seas which the Service Report described as "Very Rough", Coxswain Clegg spotted activity on the casualty's foredeck, and then saw in the water alongside the bright orange of a liferaft. Skipper McCarthy had been aware that his ship was slowly dragging her anchor in the soft sands, and ordered the raft launched as a precaution. However in the seas then running there was little hope for the tiny inflatable, and it was soon washed away and up the beach. When the "Ramsay Dyce" came up with the casualty the latter advised that the fishermen did not want to leave their vessel. Because of their draft and the sea state the tugs were unable to close the crippled trawler to pass their lines, so Coxswain

The Sixties, and The Inshore Life-boat

Clegg turned the ''Ramsay Dyce'' bow on to the surf and backed down towards the ''Ross Fortune''. As he battled to hold the life-boat's head up, his crew readied the Schermuly Line-Throwing Apparatus, and it was not long before a rocket, trailing its bright orange line, reached out over the trawler. Willing hands quickly bent on a heavier line, and the life-boat's capstan began to pull it across the intervening gap of boiling sea. Before this messenger reached the ''Ramsay Dyce'' the two vessels surged apart and the thin rocket line parted. Thrice more Leo Clegg positioned the life-boat close to the casualty, thrice more rockets were fired and lines bent on, but on each occasion they were parted by the motion.

As the life-boat manoeuvred for a fifth attempt a radio message from the tugs changed the whole complexion of the operation. They had been holding as close as they dared in very shallow water. Their constant engine movements had stirred up the bottom so much that sand had entered both vessels' engine cooling systems and their diesels had overheated. As a result both tugs had to withdraw into deeper water, well beyond the scope of any towing possibility. At this point Skipper McCarthy called the life-boat to ask, ''Can you tow us?'', and Coxswain Clegg immediately replied, ''We'll give it a go, but we'll need a heavier line than before.'' Slowly the ''Ramsay Dyce'' backed in and once again a rocket flared. This time a six inch rope followed

The trawler ''Ross Fortune'' hanging on to her anchor off the Donmouth.

the messenger to the waiting life-boat, and was made fast with considerable difficulty. In the surf the motion on board the ''Ramsay Dyce'' was unpredictable, but she was slowly eased ahead, constant helm and engine movements being necessary to keep her head to the seas. The weight came on the line, lifting it clear of the water, and almost reluctantly the ''Ross Fortune'' began to move away from the shore, her crew hauling in the anchor as she did so. Some 400 yards had been gained through the surf when the tow parted, right on the trawler's fairlead, and a thoroughly unhappy life-boat crew struggled to recover the heavy hawser, flaking it down along both sides of the casing.

By now it was dark and the lights of the two tugs were seen as they approached, engine temperatures having returned to something around normal. The ''Ramsay Dyce'' tried once more — ''This is our last rocket'', Skipper McCarthy was told, and shortly a light dan wire was being winched across to the life-boat. It was followed by one of the casualty's warps — as she was one of the first stern trawlers, this had had to be brought forward through the accommodation from right aft. ''Give us lots of slack,'' Leo Clegg told the trawlermen over the radio, and the life-boat moved slowly clear of the breakers towards the waiting ''Sea Griffon''. As soon as she could the tug came alongside the ''Ramsay Dyce'', and, not without some difficulty, the heavy warp was transferred. Soon the ''Ross Fortune'' was on the move, her anchor home, and with the tugs firmly in charge, and the Coastguard, listening on their radio heard Coxswain Clegg's last service message to the casualty, ''You're alright now, we're returning to harbour.'' By now it was 7.45pm, and by 8.30 the life-boat was back on her mooring, the tugs and the ''Ross Fortune'' having entered harbour without further incident.

The ''Ross Fortune'' safe in port after her near-stranding.

The Sixties, and The Inshore Life-boat

The big Kiel-registered trawler "Heikendorff" fought its way into Aberdeen Bay in the teeth of a whole South-easterly gale during the eveing of 12 December, 1966. Even in the lee of Girdle-ness sea conditions could only be described as "Very Rough", and the harbour itself had been closed to all shipping earlier in the day. The arrival of the German fishing vessel was not unexpected, for she radioed ahead to advise that she had a seaman with serious head injuries, and was making for the port to seek immediate medical assistance. As the harbour was closed the Port Medical Officer, Dr John Leiper, decided to go out to the "Heikendorff" in the life-boat. Taking his medical bag he boarded the "Ramsay Dyce" at Pocra Quay, and at 5.45pm Coxswain Leo Clegg steered the Barnett slowly down the navigation channel towards the wall of white water on the harbour bar.

Once clear of the treacherous sea at the entrance, Coxswain Clegg headed for the trawler. It was immediately evident that it was going to be both difficult and dangerous to transfer the doctor in the prevailing weather conditions, but the life-boat's crew were equally aware that it was vital for medical help to reach the injured man. Accordingly a full set of fenders were rigged, and the life-boat came in towards the trawler, both vessels pitching and rolling wildly in the heavy seas. It was apparent that more than a quick "touch and transfer" was going to be required, and in the event it was more than an hour before the "Ramsay Dyce" was finally in a position where the 62-year old doctor could attempt to board the "Heikendorff". As the two vessels crashed together one of the life-boatmen boosted the doctor up on to the trawler's rail where he landed heavily on his chest, and teetering — threatening to fall back on board the "Ramsay Dyce". Suddenly a huge form materialised beside the precariously-balanced medic, and Dr Leiper found himself enveloped in the arms of a gigantic German fisherman, who lifted him effortlessly over the rail and set him gently on deck. While being led to the injured fisher-man's bedside, "Dr John" felt a sharp pain in his chest and realised that he had not come unscathed through the transfer. Despite his discomfort the doctor remained with the injured man throughout the long night, for it was judged unwise to enter harbour until the wind and sea abated somewhat. The "Ramsay Dyce" meantime had worked clear of the German, and headed back towards the coast, the Coxswain setting his craft initially to the southward, and streaming the drogue to keep her stern on during the crossing of the bar. Crew members Bill Cowper and Francis Cruickshank sat in the stern compartment, tending the drogue lines. As they approached the breakwater a wall of broken water overtook the life-boat and crashed on board. The two Footdee men aft were engulfed, and clung on for dear life as the flood rushed forward, smashing into the after wheelhouse ports. Such was the water's force that it snapped the lower securing pin of one of these, and flying upwards on its hinges the heavy pane struck Second Coxswain John Martin on the back of the head. The impact threw him bodily forwards to strike his face against the windows ahead of him, but fortunately without serious injury. The sea poured into the cockpit, drenching the Coxswain at the wheel and Mechanics Ian Jack and George Walker as they crouched over their engine controls.

It was the angry sea's last fling at the life-boat, and with considerable relief they entered the somewhat calmer water of the tidal basin after the 3½ hour service. The "Heikendorff" berthed around noon the following day, the injured fisherman quickly being taken to hospital by ambulance. With him also went Dr Leiper, who found that the impact of his stormy transfer had broken several ribs.

The "Ramsay Dyce" at her Footdee moorings.

The canoeing exercise on the lower part of the River Don was seen as being something of a change from the run of the mill of Army training activity at the nearby Barracks. Five canoes, ten junior soldiers, and their NCO instructors were taking part in waterborne instruction on the afternoon of 20 June, 1967, when, literally from a clear sky, tragedy struck. Coastguard Officer Mr Bill Edwards had noted similar activity near the Bridge of Don station during previous days, but as he started his patrol that afternoon he was somewhat surprised to see the soldiers launching their small craft. A strong and gusty westerly wind was blowing the ebb tide seawards with a moderate sea kicking up quite a chop at the rivermouth. As he walked further along the bank he saw an overturned canoe lying by the south bank, with two men standing by it. Sensing instinctively that all was not well, the coastguard quickened his step and saw another canoe apparently capsized in the surf line at the river mouth. Two men were clinging to the craft's upturned hull, and the tide was rapidly carrying them out to sea. Mr Edwards turned and ran back to his station, grabbed a rocket pistol, and raced across the soft sand to find that the two men had reached a sandbank some 300 yards offshore, and were standing on it. He fired his line, but it fell short, and realising that there had been a more serious accident than he had at first suspected, he returned to call out the emergency services.

The disaster, for such it had by now become, was also seen by holiday-makers along the beach, and they initially assumed that it was all part of the exercise. When they heard the shouting, whistle blasts and the discharge of the rocket pistol they quickly realised that something was amiss and a hush fell along the shore. Figures could be seen clinging to the salmon nets to the north of the Donmouth, but one by one they seemed to disappear until only a single head remained in view. Reaction to the Coastguard's call was immediate — first on the scene was the Pilot Cutter, which immediately ran into the shallow water and picked up the sole remaining survivor from his refuge. He was an exhausted 16-year old Junior Drummer from the Highland Brigade Depot at the Barracks, and in view of his condition the Cutter made all possible speed back to port and a waiting ambulance. Hard on her heels came the "Ramsay Dyce", her crew tumbling into their gear as she reacted to the call. Close to the scene the lifeboat found and recovered three waterlogged canoes, two lifejackets and two paddles, but of the trainees there was no sign. By this time, shore parties of police, army personnel and other helpers were spreading out along the beaches on both sides of the river mouth. Naval and RAF helicopters from Lossiemouth and Leuchars also arrived, and throughout the long summer afternoon and late into the evening the search went on.

As the bright sunlight mocked the grim mood of all who took part, it became evident that two junior musicians were still missing, but apart from a further waterlogged and drifting canoe, nothing else was found. Ironically the wind went down with the sun, and as darkness fell the air search was called off. The "Ramsay Dyce" continued to search the almost-calm seas as far north as Belhelvie, then, after 7½ hours on service, she returned to her moorings, being met by police and army personnel who took away the recovered equipment.

Although the search was resumed at first light the next morning the life-boat was not initially involved, but her crew remained on standby whilst large shore parties continued their work. These latter were backed up by a Shackleton maritime patrol aircraft from RAF Kinloss, and whilst scouring the water some six miles offshore a body was found. The "Ramsay Dyce" was launched to recover it, and having been directed to the spot by the aircraft, the body of one of the missing soldiers was taken on board. For a further period the life-boat continued searching for his companion, but without success, and Coxswain Clegg returned his vessel to port after more than 4½ hours at sea. Wrapped in a blanket her tragic burden was borne gently ashore, watched by a saddened and silent crew.

Some six years after the withdrawal of the "George & Elizabeth Gow" a beach and inshore rescue capability was restored to the Aberdeen station. This followed a number of cliff-related accidents in the Gregness/Cove areas as well as the RNLI's very successful introduction of fast inflatable rescue craft to handle inshore incidents. With a crew of only two or three the craft, powered by a 40HP outboard motor, was proving ideal for the very rapid response required in beach or cliff rescues. On 21 March, 1968, it was announced that Aberdeen was to be provided with one of these inflatables, and it arrived (then designated an Inshore Rescue Boat) during August, just in time to search for a missing 3-year old girl near the Black Dog. She was found ashore some four hours later, having lost her way amongst the sand dunes, but the speed with which the new craft was able to arrive on the scene attracted much favourable comment. Initially the ILB was housed in a shed made available near the Roundhouse, and launched from the old Footdee Ferry Slipway nearby. In 1980 it was moved to the newly-built life-boat station beside the old dock gates, where a single-arm davit from a scrapped trawler had been emplaced. As a result the ILB can rapidly be put afloat and recovered at any state of the tide, and its crew can use the station's facilities.

Initially the ILB was manned by members of the life-boat's crew, but it was not long before other volunteers came forward, amongst them several police officers, members of the local force. ILB crew members tended, as they still are to this day, to be younger men, and in any case, with an upper age limit of 45 years the older life-boatmen increasingly stood down to continue with the bigger vessel. The inshore life-boat responded to a number of calls during the remainder of the 1960's and 1970's going to the aid of bathers off the Beach, or regrettably and

The Inshore Life-boat at Footdee (above) and returning to station after service with ambulancemen and casualty aboard.

more usually, dealing with the tragic and gruesome aftermath of cliff accidents to the south of the port. This area has traditionally generated a steady stream of accidents and consequent fatalities over the years, most of them involving young people skylarking on the clifftops or intent in taking eggs from the many gulls' nests around the ledges.

As most of its activity takes place in the summer months the ILB is normally stood down between the end of October and the first week of the following April. This time "off station" is

used to give the inflatable a thorough overhaul, with any defective or worn parts being replaced. As spring again approaches the annual training programme again swings into gear: in addition to its regular exercise schedule the ILB has carried out a deal of helicopter-related training work since the establishment of the first (British Airways) rescue unit at Dyce in 1971/2. The craft is also always on standby off the Beach during the course of parachute demonstrations on the nearby Queens Links.

A list of Inshore Life-boat services appears at the end of the book.

Johnny Martin, Senior, had spent all his adult life in the service of the RNLI, first as Assistance Mechanic in the old "Emma Constance" before taking over as Mechanic in the "George and Elizabeth Gow", where he remained until the No. 2 boat was withdrawn in 1962. John then returned to the No. 1 life-boat, the "Ramsay Dyce", as 2nd Coxswain with Leo Clegg. Now, in 1968, as Johnny Martin's long career drew to a close, another challenge was about to be presented to him, for after eight years as Coxswain, Leo Clegg decided to resign. He was about to move house out to Methlick and wanted to devote his spare time to the restoration of his own boat, the Loch Fyne fishing vessel "Clan Gordon", which was built in 1911. During his eight years in command, Coxswain Clegg had launched on service on forty occasions amounting to 159¼ hours at sea in all weather, and assisting 53 persons in distress.

The new Coxswain's first service in command was to the Aberdeen seine netter "Semnos II", broken down some eight miles from the port in a South Westerly gale in the late afternoon of 12th October, 1968. Hearing the fishing vessel's call for help, the Norwegian tanker "Heros" altered course to her aid and took her in tow, while "Ramsay Dyce" hastened north to stand by. After towing for about 1½ hours the tanker's towline parted in the steadily deteriorating weather and the life-boat moved in to effect a connection, some five miles from Cruden Scaurs. At 8.05pm the "Ramsay Dyce's" line was finally secured − an extremely hazardous operation in the storm − and Coxswain Martin began the run to safety. He chose Peterhead, as it was obvious that to attempt to make Aberdeen against the fury of the gale would be bound to fail, with the drag of the seiner astern. The two ships duly entered the "Blue Toon", and the "Semnos II" was made fast. The life-boat then made the storm-tossed passage back to her station, entering harbour at 2.50am on the thirteenth.

To the end of the decade "Ramsay Dyce" and the relief life-boat "Southern Africa" (provided by the donations of the South African Branch of the Institution) launched on six more occasions, spending 21 hours at sea on service. During this period Motor Mechanic Iain Jack served as acting 2nd Coxswain until, once again, another boat officer was found from outside the crew.

Albert Bird, Manager of a George Street electrical appliance shop, was the final choice for the position. At sea for many years in the Merchant Navy, Albert had good cause to be pleased when he was invited to join the crew as 2nd Coxswain. Some twelve years previously, while second mate, his ship was capsized in the English Channel in a storm. Albert spent over an hour in the freezing water before he was rescued — by the Dungeness Life-boat!

Johnny Martin stayed on as Coxswain until 1972 when he retired from the Service he had served so faithfully for so long, and Albert Bird was confirmed in the position of Coxswain.

Coxswain Albert Bird and crew.

The Early Seventies

The night of Friday, 4 January, 1974, was unpleasant even by local winter standards, with a near-storm force Southerly wind driving a huge sea along the Kincardine and Aberdeenshire coasts. Early that evening members of the Murcar Golf Club were enjoying a drink in the warmth of the bar when they were startled by the sudden arrival of two bedraggled seamen who literally fell through the door. Their lack of English made explanations difficult, but it very soon became obvious that a ship was ashore on the nearby sands, and the word was quickly passed via the police to the emergency services. The Life-boat's Hon Secretary, Captain Brian Atkinson, was informed at around 6.15pm, and he immediately began calling out the crew.

The life of a harbour boatman can be extremely unpleasant, and may entail waiting in all weathers for the slow approach of an inbound vessel, handling cold and sodden lines, or moving around the port in an open boat. One such occasion was this night of 4 January, with the life-boat's Assistant Mechanic George Walker, and Bowman William Cowper having just moored a large Polish trawler. The pilot was still on board, and as the two boatmen, heads bowed against the storm-driven rain, passed him he called down, "George, Billy, there's another Pole aground at Murcar — the Skipper here's just heard it on the VHF!" Realising that the life-boat was almost certain to be involved, the two ran for their boat and made all possible speed across the tidal basin to the "Ramsay Dyce". Remaining crew members soon tumbled on board, and at 6.40pm the big Barnett, with Coxswain Albert Bird at the wheel, left her moorings.

The Polish steam trawler "Nurzec" had apparently earlier been waiting to enter harbour, dodging up and down, and falling too far back had been driven bodily ashore by the sheer force of the wind. Two crew members then launched a dinghy, but had covered less than 200 of the 400 yards of boiling surf to the beach when their little craft was capsized and they were forced to swim and wade the rest of the way. It was their dramatic arrival at the Murcar club which provided the first indication of the late-afternoon drama.

The various rescue services quickly swung into action, but it was at this point, as help was on its way to the scene by land and sea, that fate took a hand and tragedy struck. Possibly unaware of British rescue facilities and procedures, or perhaps as Eastern Bloc shipping is wont to do by keeping incidents "in the family", the Russian tug "Gordiy" arrived to seaward of the casualty. She then launched one of her open life-boats into the raging seas with a crew of five seamen, and they did very well to reach the stranded trawler. No less than 18 of the remaining Polish fishermen scrambled into the frail craft, but within minutes it was capsized and all 23 occupants were thrown into the sea.

The "Ramsay Dyce" arrived on the scene at 6.40pm, but owing to the huge breaking seas and the lack of water inshore, was unable to approach the "Nurzec" without joining her on the sands. At about the same time a British Airways Sikorsky S-61N helicopter was scrambled from Dyce airport on the company's first night SAR mission. Albert Bird took the life-boat across to the Russian tug, intending to discover exactly what was going on, and as he tried to make contact across the heaving waters, the wind began to ease off somewhat. However, no-one on the tug made any response to repeated radio or loudhailer calls, and this continued even when the "Ramsay Dyce" took the risky course of going alongside the Soviet vessel.

On the beach, meanwhile, men were scrambling from the water, with nine actually making it to the Murcar club house, where the rescue agencies had established a temporary command centre. Five more were dragged out of the sea and rushed by ambulance to the Royal Infirmary, and another four were found to be dead in the upturned life-boat as it lay in the surf. The use of the helicopter to search along the coast proved totally successful as its crew spotted and

Aftermath of tragedy — the Polish trawler "Nurzec" aground off Murcar.

Abandoned liferafts lie in mute testimony to the "Nurzec" disaster.

recovered a single survivor about a mile distant from the scene. The aircraft's lights went on to illuminate the more remote parts of the sand dunes for any other castaways, whilst the lifeboat's crew sent up parachute flares to help the shore parties.

Although the Coastguard eventually managed to fire a rocket line on board, no further response was obtained from the casualty. In consequence, and after some discussion, it was decided that there was no point in the ''Ramsay Dyce'' remaining at sea, so she thankfully made her way back to port, being refuelled and ready for further service by 1.05am on 5 January. However, she was not required later that day when the remaining Poles were winched from the stranded trawler by helicopter, and there only remained an official expression of unhappiness over inexplicable aspects of the night's events. In a well-attended press conference the local Coastguard chief strongly expressed the view that had the Russians been more co-operative, there would have been no need for them to launch their boat against impossible odds. The stranded fishermen could then have been taken off in the morning by helicopter or breeches buoy, but the whole matter left something of an unpleasant taste amongst the local maritime community. This was especially true of Albert Bird and his crew, all of whom were dumbfounded over their cavalier treatment by the Russians.

Sightseers visit the ''Nurzec'' after the tragedy.

The 268-ton Leith-registered trawler "Netta Croan" left Granton on the morning of 13 April, 1974, and headed out of the Firth of Forth, bound once again for the northern fishing grounds. By nightfall her crew had shaken down into their normal passage routine, and some five miles on his port beam Skipper John Rutherford could see the lights of Aberdeen twinkling in the clear night air, with the beam of Girdleness light sweeping across the calm sea. Even at her cruising speed of nine knots the trawler's bow wave was impressive, gleaming blue-white in the spring darkness as she forged northwards. In the vessel's galley the Chief Engineer and 18-year old Harry Cummings laboured to repair the main cooking stove. Suddenly, it "blew back", oil fuel spraying the compartment, then igniting and engulfing it in flames. Extinguishers, water and buckets of sand were all tried but without avail, and so rapid was the spread of the outbreak that there was insufficient time for the fire pumps to be started.

Swiftly the tranquility of the night was shattered, and up in the wheelhouse the 66-year old skipper, with less than 12 months to go before retirement, remained at his radio to transmit distress calls until the flames began eating their way through the very deck planking around him. Finding his way aft blocked by a sea of fire, Skipper Rutherford climbed out through a forward wheelhouse window, and joined his shocked 12-man crew, soon being forced on the fo'c'sle by the heat and fumes. Gregness coastguard station had picked up the distress messages, and it was not long before phones were ringing amongst the rescue agencies. The big British Airways S-61N helicopter on SAR standby at Dyce airport was quickly towed out of its hangar whilst its pilots and crewmen responded to the call and left their homes with all possible speed. Meanwhile, Captain Atkinson, the Hon Secretary, was experiencing some difficulty due to congestion on the local telephone system. Finally he succeeded in making contact, and Coxswain Albert Bird, Mechanic Ian Jack, Assistant Mechanic George Walker and crewmen Francis Cruickshank and Andrew Walker, made their several hasty ways to the harbour. Initially the Coastguard had requested the life-boat to go on standby, but when the crew arrived at Footdee the situation off the coast had deteriorated to the extent that an 'immediate launch' was requested. At 9.30pm the relief life-boat "Hilton Briggs", (by now fitted with an enclosed wheelhouse), slipped her moorings and proceeded at full speed towards the flaring red glow on the northward horizon.

On board the "Netta Croan" the scene was by now almost indescribable, the wheelhouse structure a skeleton amongst the flames, whilst in places even the deck plates were melting in the heat. The 13 fishermen huddled together up forward, unable to do more than watch the fire devour their vessel as it was impossible either to stop the engine or steer her. As a result the trawler careered wildly at full speed in a gigantic circle to starboard − when she turned into the gentle night breeze the flames roared some 50 feet into the air, and thick black smoke poured from the devastated accommodation. Then tragedy added itself to the disaster as three of the trawlermen succeeded in putting an inflatable liferaft over the side, to trail on its painter, hard against the vessel's side. A 34-year old Edinburgh deck-hand, Hugh Farrell, dropped down into it, but at nine knots the sudden weight on one side was too much, and it twisted to throw its canopy against the hull plating, with Farrell vanishing into the sea. Skipper Rutherford then told his remaining crew to stay on board, his fear of an explosion should the flames reach the fuel tanks only being superseded by that of his men being spread over a wide area of the dark sea.

By this time the "Netta Croan" was not alone in her ordeal, with the naval vessel "Loyal Proctor" and the oil rig supply vessel "Smit Lloyd 47" at hand, each trying in vain to put rocket lines on board the casualty. Then, with a clatter of rotor blades the British Airways S-61N helicopter arrived, powerful lights blazing as the pilot skilfully manoeuvred the big machine into position so that he could lower his winchman. His task was far from easy as he had to follow the crazy gyrations of the seemingly-demented trawler with a precision which would permit of the winchman being lowered through the tangle of strays and fishing gear rigged in the forward part of the ship. Three times he tried it, and three times, to the frustration of Winchman George Edge, he was forced to abort as the trawler swung off course and threatened to engulf everything in its funeral pyre.

As the aircraft stood off after its last attempt to formate on the "Netta Croan", the lifeboat arrived and set off in pursuit of the casualty. The latter was still following her erratic course to starboard, slowing and speeding up as the flames ate at her control mechanism. One report gives the speed as increasing to 14 knots, but even with both throttles hard against their stops the 24-year old "Hilton Briggs" could only make nine knots. After a fruitless interval spent in chasing the trawler from right astern, the life-boatmen held a brief 'council of war', for they intuitively felt that time was running out. Coxswain Bird put his wheel to starboard and headed across the inside of the circle as a means of catching up. He then made a further shrewd decision − Ian Jack, the 41-year old Mechanic had spent some time in charge of pilot boats and so was well experienced in going alongside moving vessels. He took the wheel, and the Coxswain took up position in the wheelhouse doorway to guide him in. Assistant Mechanic

Survivors of the trawler "Netta Croan" come ashore.

The Early Seventies

George Walker took over the engine controls, whilst Francis Cruikshank and Andrew Walker went on to the foredeck to receive survivors.

As the "Hilton Briggs" approached the noise was tremendous, with the crackling roar of the flames, the thunder of the life-boat's diesels, and the clatter of the helicopter, all making speech impossible. It was, however, unnecessary, for as the life-boat came through the thick black smoke Ian Jack straightened her up just six feet clear of the burning ship. Then, with a half-turn of the wheel the 52-foot life-boat ran delicately alongside, to lie between the forward gallows and the break of the forecastle. In less than four minutes the trawlermen had scrambled to safety, and another half-turn of the wheel took the "Hilton Briggs" clear of the inferno. Leaving the "Netta Croan" to charge off into the night, the life-boat returned to port to turn the survivors into the care of the Fishermen's Mission, and at 11.50pm, with coffee and sandwiches put on board, returned to search for the missing man. At 2.15am the following morning this was called off, to be resumed again at daylight, but without success despite a further four

Still smouldering, the "Netta Croan" lies in Aberdeen harbour.

122

hours on service. Later that day the "Netta Croan" was taken in tow by the tug "Euroman", and still smouldering, was brought into Aberdeen.

In recognition of their efforts, the RNLI awarded both Coxswain Albert Bird and Motor Mechanic Ian Jack the Institution's Silver Medal for Gallantry, these decorations being presented in London on 8th May, 1975 by HRH the Duke of Kent.

Medal winners from the "Netta Croan" service. Left to right: Ian Jack, Albert Bird, Francis Cruickshank, George Walker (extreme right).

The New Era-R.N.L.B. `BP FORTIES´

The changes evident in Aberdeen as the city assumed the role of Europe's oil capital during the mid 1970's were no more apparent than in the marine context. More and more supply ships, tugs, and vessels of weird appearance and function were seen in the port, whilst in the air helicopters became as regular a part of the local scene as buses as they shuttled men and equipment to and from the rigs and platforms offshore. The special blend of skills and capabilities of these machines and their crews in the marine rescue role were particularly well demonstrated in the "Netta Croan" service; helicopters are now an integral part of the search and rescue organisation around our coasts, indeed many assume that rotary-wing aircraft have taken over from life-boats, but helicopter crews are amongst the first to stress that each element has its place in sea rescue, as was borne out during the "Netta Croan" incident.

By 1975 the "Ramsay Dyce" was 15 years old, and with word of the RNLI having developed newer and faster vessels, it was inevitable that local thoughts began to turn towards a replacement. Perhaps with this in mind, the visit to the port that year of the first "Arun" class life-boat aroused more than a passing interest. Most of the Aberdeen crew took the opportunity of going to sea in the new vessel and they must have been impressed, for a movement to

Aberdeen Lifeboatmen of the 1970's. Left to right: Ian Jack, George Walker, Charles Begg, Bill Cowper, Coxswain Albert Bird, Andrew Walker and Francis Cruickshank.

provide an "Arun" for Aberdeen was soon in full swing. Driving force behind the fund-raising effort was then Branch Hon Secretary (Finance) Ron Addison, who faced the enormous challenge of raising some £240,000 to defray building costs. In the interim the RNLI allocated the fifth "Arun" (54-05) to the Aberdeen station, and early in 1976 Motor Mechanic Ian Jack went to Littlehampton to standby the vessel during the latter part of her construction.

Whilst he was thus engaged the "Ramsay Dyce" was again on service, this time as a bystander whilst the helicopter element of the local rescue "partnership" carried out the text-book recovery of 17 men from one of Richard Irvine's trawlers, the "Ben Gulvain", which had stranded some 200 yards offshore the 15th fairway of the Royal Aberdeen Club's course at the Bridge of Don. The life-boat launched into the teeth of a Force 9 SE gale and very rough seas just after 12.45pm on 29 January, 1976. The big trawler had suffered engine failure shortly after sailing from Aberdeen and her distress call was initially answered by the harbour tug "Sea Griffon". However, there was only time for one pass before the casualty took the ground and

One of the crew of the trawler "Ben Gulvain" being rescued by an Aberdeen-based British Airways S-61N helicopter.

The New Era – R.N.L.B. "BP Forties"

the line parted almost immediately. At this point the tug's propellor began to kick up sand from the bottom and she was forced to withdraw to deeper water.

The "Ben Gulvain" lay with her bows up the beach and her stern taking the full force of the big, breaking seas. Although she was well aground and with no sign of a list, her crew launched two life rafts into the surf, only to be told on the radio by Coxswain Albert Bird to stay on board and not to risk the wildly-tossing inflatables. The Coastguard agreed, and indicated that the trawlermen would be brought ashore by breeches buoy. Attempts to fire rocket lines across the stranded trawler were unsuccessful due to the wind, and eventually the now familiar British Airways S-6IN helicopter was called out. It was not long before the trawlermen were being winched to safety and taken, several at a time, to the golf course car park. The "Ramsay Dyce" was stood down and returned to her station at 4.30pm. "Ben Gulvain" was eventually refloated and towed down to Anstruther in Fife to be part of the museum there. Unfortunately she broke loose in a storm, doing a great deal of damage to vessels and the surrounding quays. Following this episode, the ill-fated trawler was scrapped.

"Ben Gulvain" ashore at the
Bridge of Don.

Efforts were in the meantime continuing to raise money for the new life-boat, and on 20 February, 1976, the local press reported that British Petroleum had agreed to donate the huge sum of £100,000 towards part of the cost. It was also announced that, in recognition of the company's generosity, the new vessel would be named ''RNLB BP Forties''. A further £7,000 was later donated by the 1976 Student Charities Campaign to defray some of the cost of the new life-boat's electrical equipment. Delivery was promised for the Summer of 1976, but Aberdeen had not yet finished with the ''Ramsay Dyce'' for on 12 March she performed an outstanding service which was to earn a well-deserved Bronze Medal for her Second Coxswain.

The duty officer at Aberdeen Harbour's Roundhouse watched the sturdy fishing vessel pass his position during the early evening of 12 March, 1976. As he followed her course down the navigation channel he saw her start to lift to the moderate swell running into the port, and as her lights moved away eastwards, he entered her details in his departure log. ''Karemma'', of Leith, outward bound after bunkering. From Claybank, 70 boxes on board, now bound Granton, Sailed Aberdeen . . .'' He glanced up to see the trawler was taking some time to clear the bar, and then the radio crackled, ''Harbour Radio, Karemma. I've got a problem, our steering has packed up and we're out of control . . .'' His log forgotten, the duty officer acknowledged the trawler's call and reached urgently for the telephone. In seconds he was through to the Coastguard, and shortly thereafter he heard their Duty Controller talking to the casualty on the radio.

Notified by the Roundhouse, the harbour tug ''Sea Trojan'' proceeded down-channel in pursuit of the ''Karemma', by now being swept to the northwards as had the ''Ben Gulvain'' only some six weeks earlier. Meanwhile the life-boat crew had been called out, and at 6.55pm the ''Ramsay Dyce'' slipped her mooring and in turn hastened out to sea. It had not been possible to contact Coxswain Albert Bird as he was in transit between his office and his home, so Second Coxswain Charles Begg was at the wheel. In the interim the tug had managed to get a heaving line on board the crippled trawler, but before the towline could be passed the lighter rope parted. An attempt to come alongside was now made, but the heavy seas set the casualty heavily down on the tug, to carry away most of the trawler's maindeck guardrails. At this point the ''Sea Trojan'' drew off, and Second Coxswain Begg brought the life-boat in for his first look at the situation. Assistant Motor Mechanic George Walker described the scene, ''It was like an

The New Era – R.N.L.B. ''BP Forties''

empty oil drum being driven by the seas, rolling her right over, then she'd come up again — great big white seas sweeping right across the Bay. I remember wondering, ''How are we going to get close enough to that thing to do any good?''

The trawler's skipper, 27-year old Ernest Watt Jnr, contacted the ''Ramsay Dyce'' on the radio, and asked for a line to turn his vessel into the sea. Coxswain Begg explained that the life-boat would very likely be in peril of being dragged over by the ''Karemma'' if this were to be attempted and suggested that the crew should come off before the trawler stranded. The Skipper agreed, and the ''Ramsay Dyce'' approached; as she slid under the casualty's lee a huge rolling sea swept the trawler down on to the life-boat. A wall of water poured on board, into both the wheelhouse and cabin, to put all the radios out of action. Clear of the ''Karemma'', by now very close to the shore, and without communications of any kind, the life-boat squared up down-sea from the trawler. On the latter came, swept before the swell, and hurtling down on the life-boat. Just as it seemed as if the ''Ramsay Dyce '' would be run down, a ''cushion'' of water rose between the two vessels, and for a moment they lay together. Two fishermen scrambled on board and as they were taken to the shelter of the cabin, the craft were thrown apart once more.

The trawler ''Karemma'' aground on Aberdeen Beach.

Only Skipper Watt was left on board the "Karemma", and his 61-year old father, who had been sailing with his son on this fateful trip watched anxiously as the life-boat made yet another approach, touched, and backed off with the last man on board. As the "Ramsay Dyce" worked her way clear of the surf the trawler finally struck, not more than five minutes after her skipper had been snatched to safety.

With the drogue steamed to keep her stern on to the seas breaking on the bar, the "Ramsay Dyce" entered port, and was back on her moorings by 8.10pm. Skipper Watt and his crew went off to the Fishermen's Mission for a hot meal, and having completed refuelling, it

In improving weather, "Karemma" awaits the salvors.

was not long before the life-boatmen were also back at their homes. In recognising the difficulties of this service the RNLI announced that Acting Coxswain Charles Begg had been awarded the Institution's Bronze Medal for Gallantry, for ''Showing great courage, determination and seamanship in overcoming the hazardous conditions to effect a successful rescue.'' In addition, the Institution's Thanks on Vellum was awarded to Motor Mechanic Ian Jack, whilst medal certificates were given to Assistant Motor Mechanic George Walker, Bowman William Cowper and crew members Francis Cruickshank and Andrew Walker.

The ''Karemma'' comes free of the sands — only to strand (permanently) off the Ythan a few days later.

Tuesday, 1 June, 1976, began as an untypical early summer day, with heavy rain in the morning, patchy fog, and below-average temperatures. However, the early afternoon saw the beginnings of a clearance, and by teatime conditions were perfect. Large crowds began to gather on both sides of the navigation channel to watch as a cavalcade of vessels put to sea in line astern — the life-boat "Ramsay Dyce", the ILB, the two harbour tugs, the pilot cutter, and in a much-appreciated gesture, Aberdeen University RN Unit's inshore minesweeper, HMS Thornham, carrying many members of life-boatmen's families.

The flotilla altered course to the southward, and as they rounded Girdleness, they saw another vessel, an enormous bow wave on each side of her deep blue hull as she approached. The bright orange superstructure caught the sun as Coxswain Albert Bird brought Aberdeen's new "Arun" class life-boat to join the waiting vessels, and there was a brief pause whilst the "Ramsay Dyce" carefully went alongside to transfer the city's Lord and Lady Provost. The vessels again formed into line ahead, and with the brand-new "BP Forties" in the lead, they shaped up for the navigation channel.

As part of the welcome, Coastguards had stationed themselves along the approach road and North Pier, and the sky was soon full of parachute flares of all colours as they burst overhead in salute. Whilst the crowd may not have been as large as that on hand to greet the Royal

The "BP Forties" enters Aberdeen for the first time.

The New Era – R.N.L.B. "BP Forties"

Yacht "Britannia", the police reported that thousands of people had turned out, a measure of the respect in which the RNLI is held locally. After mooring at Footdee, those of the crew who had not been on delivery voyage were quick to inspect their new life-boat. Technically, she was about as far advanced from her predecessor as the "Emma Constance" had been over the old pre-RNLI pulling boats. "BP Forties" is 53′ 5¾″ in overall length with a 17-foot beam and a depth of 7 feet. Twin turbo-blown Caterpillar diesels each of 460 hp give her a speed of almost 19 knots, for a full-power range of some 220 nautical miles. Her self-righting capability stems from her inherent buoyancy, much of which results from her enclosed cabin layout. Provided this is intact she will right herself in less than nine seconds. All essential controls, such as wheel, throttles, etc, are duplicated on the flying bridge, and each of her six-man crew is provided with an aircraft-type seat, this complete with safety harness. An inflatable "daughter boat" is carried on top of the cabin for inshore work, and was initially launched over the side by means of a derrick (this is now done over the stern with a winch and portable launching spars). All this made an immense impression on the Aberdeen crew, who took an immediate pride in their new vessel, and went on to carry out numerous exercises to familiarise themselves with its considerable capabilities.

Aberdeen Branch Hon Secretary (Finance) and present Chairman Rodney Addison OBE, with the part-completed "BP Forties" in the background.

R.N.L.B. BP Forties undergoing capsize trials at Cowes, Isle of Wight, 1975. 1, "Over she goes", the lifeboat is deliberately capsized. 2, BP Forties rests briefly on the cabin casing before (3,4) self-righting occurs. 5, Back on an even keel the BP Forties passes the test.

The New Era – R.N.L.B. "BP Forties"

The new life-boat's first service took place on 28 July, 1976, in response to a distress call from the fishing vessel "Westerdale", reporting that she was taking water some 50nm off Girdleness. Owned by the Don Fishing Company of Aberdeen, and with a crew of seven, the trawler had been on its way to the fishing grounds when water was discovered pouring into the engine room. Skipper R B Malcolm turned his vessel back towards Aberdeen, had the pumps started, and sent out a MAYDAY call, this including information that difficulty was being experienced in controlling the flooding. The trawler's message was picked up by the Coastguard, and at 2.55am the "BP Forties" left port. The night was clear, with a moderate NNW breeze, so Coxswain Bird was easily able to open his throttles and allow the twin 460BHP Caterpillar diesels to drive the life-boat through the choppy seas at almost 19 knots. The "BP Forties" came up with the casualty at 4.47am, and another new piece of equipment was immediately brought into use. By now the trawler's pumps had failed, but the life-boat was able to transfer her portable pump to contain the flooding during the return to Aberdeen. Both vessels docked at around 9.00am that morning after a service lasting just over six hours, and one which would have taken much longer with previous life-boats.

At 3.30pm on 9 September, 1976, two maroons exploded in the grey skies above Aberdeen Harbour – the traditional signal used around British coasts to summon life-boat crews to their stations. However, that day they marked an occasion of less gravity although the Granite City's attention was still centred around a life-boat. Dressed overall with signal flags, the deep blue and bright orange Arun lay in the Upper Dock, moored bows on to Regent Quay for her naming and dedication ceremony. The Band of the Royal Marines (Flag Officer Scotland & N Ireland) provided suitable music as Coxswain Albert Bird, Second Coxswain Charles Begg, Motor Mechanic Ian Jack, Assistant Motor Mechanic George Walker, Bowman William Cowper, and crew members Francis Cruickshank and John Corstorphine, stood proudly on the well-scrubbed foredeck facing the official party. Alongside lay the Inshore life-boat, and the proceedings were watched by a considerable crowd. The ceremony's highlight was the new boat's naming by Mrs (now Lady) Ann Steel, wife of the then Chairman of British Petroleum, who pressed a button to smash the traditional bottle of champagne against the vessel's bows. Following the formal part of the afternoon's events the platform party went on board the "BP Forties", which then put to sea for a brief trip round the Bay.

It was back to business on 1 October, 1976, when, at 4.10am, Captain Atkinson, the Hon Secretary, was awakened by a telephone call from the Coastguard, informing him that they had

just intercepted a radio conversation between the oil standby vessel (converted trawler) "Sherrifmuir" and the Roundhouse. The former had reported that she was ashore on the beach in thick fog some three miles to the north of the port, and to seaward of the Murcar Golf Clubhouse. Life-boat assistance was requested, but when the "BP Forties" arrived on the scene Coxswain Bird soon realised that he would be unable to close the casualty due to the shallow water and the heavy breaking seas running up the beach. As a result the vessel's crew were advised to remain on board, and at low water the salmon fishermen's tractor and trailer went out to take them off. The "Sherrifmuir" however, was to remain on the sands for much longer, not being removed until 1984, when as part of a wreck clearance programme, her rusting hulk was cut up for scrap.

One year later to the day, the "BP Forties" was launched into a very rough sea to proceed to a position some 48nm ENE of Aberdeen, where a Bristow's Sikorsky S-61N helicopter with three men on board had ditched following mechanical trouble. The life-boat smashed her way towards the scene for over an hour before being recalled when a British Airways rescue aircraft recovered the capsized machine's crew.

Only seven services were carried out between 1977 and 1980, six of these by the "BP

The New Era – R.N.L.B. ''BP Forties''

Forties'', and the other by the relief life-boat ''John Gellatly Hyndman''. On one occasion (14 January, 1977) the Arun class's flexibility was very well demonstrated when the Aberdeen vessel was called to assist two anglers cut off by the tide at Girdleness. Unable to come in close enough, the inflatable ''daughter boat'' was launched and within minutes had the two fishermen on board from the rocks where they were marooned.

During this period Coxswain Bird indicated that he would be retiring when a suitable successor was appointed. Second Coxswain Charles Begg had only recently resigned, so Albert's ''run-down'' period was to be somewhat protracted, and it was not until May, 1980, that Divisional Life-boat Inspector Chris Price, who had been literally scouring the city for candidates brought three prospective crew members on exercise. As all of them were involved in the oil industry, it was decided that the ideal solution would be to appoint a coxswain and two second coxswains. In theory at any rate this would result in at least two boat officers being available at any time. Norman Trewren,* an ex-Merchant Navy Officer became Coxswain-elect, whilst James Dickson (also ex-Merchant Service), and David Mitchell (ex-Royal Navy) were to be the new second coxswains. Before this, however, ''BP Forties'' was called out yet again.

*(Author's note: I well remember the day Chris Price stuck his head round my office door and said, ''I'm looking for volunteers for the life-boat.'' I duly volunteered, but it was not until that first exercise that I realised he was looking, not for crew members, but for a coxswain!)

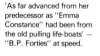

'As far advanced from her predecessor as ''Emma Constance'' had been from the old pulling life-boats' — ''B.P. Forties'' at speed.

1980-1985

The evening of 22 February, 1980, was calm, but with a dense fog cutting visibility almost to nil across the heavy swell rolling into the port. It was so thick that the Roundhouse watchkeepers were barely able to see across the navigation channel, and shipping movements could only be monitored on radar. At about 8.45pm the 40-foot fishing vessel "Norfolk Spinner" called up on VHF radio to request permission to enter harbour. Watching on his radar the Roundhouse duty officer warned the MFV that it was too far south, and should alter course to the northward. A tanker movement then occupied the harbour staff's attention, but very shortly after they were horrified to hear the fishing vessel's engineer, Terry Watson, calling to say that the "Norfolk Spinner" had gone to the ledge on the seaward side of the South Breakwater, and was now breaking up under the pounding of the swells as they smashed shorewards.

The local rescue services were immediately alerted, with Police, Fire and Ambulance vehicles swiftly on the scene, having made their way along Greyhope Road to the inner end of the breakwater. As they did so, the "BP Forties" left port, and having felt her way through the blanketing fog, arriving off the casualty's reported position at 9.10pm. Approaching as close as they dared, the life-boatmen scoured the fog, but without success, and then having been advised from the shore that the "Norfolk Spinner" was stranded on the root of the breakwater, they soon realised that afloat assistance could only be minimal. Nevertheless, the daughter boat with motor mechanic Ian Jack and bowman Bill Cowper aboard, was launched to attempt an approach. It very soon become obvious that even this effort was doomed to failure in the prevailing conditions, and the only hope for the fishermen now lay with the shore parties, just 15 feet above the disintegrating "Norfolk Spinner".

By this time two of the three men on board the casualty seem to have been washed over-board into the surf, and only the engineer now remained in the flooded wheelhouse. The Fire Service, ignoring the possible risk posed by the seas pouring over the breakwater, took a turntable ladder along it, and Coastguard officer Peter R. Capper volunteered to be lowered to the wreck. In the glare of the floodlights the engineer was just visible in the tiny wheelhouse, and the Coastguard, swinging in his harness, had to smash its windows before he could reach the survivor. Already the effects of cold and shock had brought Watson to a state in which he could neither help himself nor speak to his rescuer, so a second coastguard, Station Officer John Rainford, went on board to assist his colleague. With their combined efforts the comatose engineer was lifted clear, and his two rescuers were recovered before their own positions became untenable. An ambulance rushed Watson to hospital, where he underwent urgent treatment for hypothermia. Unfortunately this proved unsuccessful, and despite everything the medical team could do for him, he died some hours later. It was not long, too, before it had to be accepted that despite an intensive search by the life-boat and the fishing vessel "Contender", his two companions were also lost. After almost three hours spent in fruitlessly quartering the turbulence generated by the swell and rising tide around the harbour entrance, the "BP Forties" was stood down and returned to her station.

For their courage in extremely hazardous conditions the two Coastguards were later decorated with the Queen's Commendation for Brave Conduct.

British Airways Helicopters' flight "Zero Seven Golf" was inbound from the oil rig "Atlantic II" on the morning of 31 July, 1980, when at around 12.00 noon, and some 60 nautical miles ESE of Aberdeen, the two pilots became aware of a mechanical problem. There was a decrease in transmission oil pressure, and an increase in its temperature, both of these showing a significant divergence from the normal. Captain David Paul radioed Dyce airport to alert rescue agencies and then brought the big Sikorsky S-61N down to a lower altitude. A Royal Air Force Shackleton aircraft on patrol nearby altered course to close the helicopter's flight path, and as the transmission's condition continued to deteriorate — one oil cooler belt having failed and fouled the other — a decision was made to land the S-61N on the sea. This was in accordance with the company's operational policy, and a manoeuvre regularly practised by oil-support aircrew. The 13 passengers were alerted, and at approximately 12.20pm BA Helicopter G-BEID made a successful "power-on" water landing. By this time the aircraft was some 24 nautical miles from Aberdeen airport, and weather conditions included light winds, a slight swell, but poor visibility in low cloud and patchy sea fog.

Due to this swell, estimated at between three and five feet in height, the aircraft rolled heavily during the course of attempts to taxy it shorewards, and as indications of mechanical trouble grew, both engines had to be shut down. The sea anchor was then streamed, but the rolling continued to a level at which the Captain ordered his co-pilot and passengers into one of the aircraft's two inflatable dinghies.

(Ashore it was a lovely day, so much so that the author decided not to wait until the following morning before setting off with his family on their annual holiday. In consequence, and just as Captain Atkinson, the Hon Secretary, was alerting the life-boat crew to "India Delta's" plight, the Trewren clan set off, thereby missing what would otherwise have been the

The occupants of the ditched British Airways S-61N are winched on board a rescue helicopter as the aircraft is towed to port by the "BP Forties".

writer's first actual service!)

As it happened, the "BP Forties" put to sea at 12.25pm with Second Coxswain Jim Dickson in command, and ran at full speed through thick fog patches and visibility at times of less than 100 yards, to reach the scene shortly after 1.30pm. By now several other vessels were in the immediate area, and a winch-fitted Bristow S-61N arrived to lift eight of the passengers from the life raft. The remainder were taken on board the life-boat, together with their raft, which was deflated and stowed away. The Shackleton had been of considerable value in homing rescue helicopters to the scene, and its pictures showing the ditched helicopter with the ''BP Forties'' in close proximity were widely published in the national press.

Because of the calm conditions and improving visibility it was decided to tow the aircraft back to port, its boat-shaped hull being the major incentive for this course of action. A BAH engineer had been winched on board the life-boat, and motor mechanic Ian Jack took him across to the downed S-61N in the daughter boat. There a life raft was inflated inside the cabin to improve buoyancy in the event of of capsize. Doors were again closed, air bags were secured above the sponsons to increase stability, and a tow line was bent on to the sea anchor painter. Very carefully the life-boat went ahead, working slowly up to a speed of some three knots, and good progress was soon being made towards the shore. Meanwhile the Bristow aircraft had picked up the helicopter's remaining passengers and two pilots, and took them to hospital in Aberdeen for a checkup.

Details of the successful ditching had been the subject of very considerable TV, radio, and press coverage, so large crowds jammed every vantage point some six hours later as the ''BP

The ditched helicopter safely in Aberdeen harbour.

Forties'', together with her unique burden, prepared to enter harbour at around 7.00pm. The towline was shortened in at the harbour mouth, and despite a slight increase in rolling as the bar was crossed, this phase of the operation passed without problem. Abeam of the Roundhouse the tow was again shortened, and the life-boat's inflatable was launched to take a line to the helicopter's tail boom to keep it under greater control during the last stage of the recovery.

The Inshore Life-boat keeps the helicopter clear of the quayside.

The ILB had been launched not long before to assist, and hundreds of cameras recorded the scene in the evening sunlight as G-BEID was eased alongside one of the deepwater berths. A gentle southerly breeze threatened to blow the aircraft's fragile rotor blades against the concrete as preparations were made for a crane lift, so the ILB moved in (the daughter boat had been released). Its helmsman took careful hold of a projecting tailboom aerial, and with gentle applications of throttle, moved the aircraft clear. The ILB had previously put a BAH engineer on board the helicopter and he passed a long heavy-duty nylon strop around the rotor head. A harbour crane was already in position, and a few moments later the S-61N was swung ashore for specialist inspection and washing down with fresh water. In all this service lasted for almost 7 ½ hours, and so little damage had been done to the aircraft that it was flying again in less than a week.

A Shackleton aircraft of No.8 Sqn. RAF.

The author's first service on board the "BP Forties" took place on 8 August, 1980, and involved the fishing vessel "Shannon", reported as taking water some 26nm ENE of Aberdeen. With Coxswain Bird at the helm, the life-boat sailed at about 7.00am, and once the portable pump and mechanic had been transferred to the casualty, it was a case of escorting her as she was towed shorewards by the fishing vessel "Boy Steven". The fresh SW wind was raising a moderate sea when it became obvious that the life-boat's pump could not cope with the inflow, and accordingly, a Sea King helicopter from RAF Lossiemouth brought out a larger unit which was winched on board. This effectively solved the problem and both vessels entered port just before 4.00pm that afternoon, closely followed by the "BP Forties".

This proved to be Albert Bird's last service, for at the next call-out, on 28 September, 1980, the author ran down the pontoon gangway shortly before 1.00am, and observing the crew letting go the last of the mooring lines, he asked innocently, "Where's Albert?", receiving the short reply, "You're Albert, chum, let's go!". They went, the reason for this call being a report of an overdue cabin cruiser which had left Cove for Stonehaven early the previous evening with only the one man on board. It was a beautiful night, clear, and with a calm sea and little wind, but although the life-boat and two fast rescue craft from RGIT's Stonehaven Maritime Rescue Section searched the area thoroughly, nothing was found. It was not until daybreak that the missing craft was discovered by an RAF helicopter off Inverbervie. Taken in tow to Stonehaven by the life-boat, it emerged that the casualty had run out of fuel, therefore had no lights, and in addition no flares, and no means of communication!

The next service, on 19 December, 1980, was a very different experience, with a SSE wind blowing at between Force 7 and 8, and heaping heavy seas on to the Beach when the BUT standby vessel "Ross Khartoum" left port for the Brent Field. Some seven miles off her engineers encountered problems with the big converted trawler's power plant, and Skipper Jack Stephen accordingly decided to return to harbour. Then the engine stopped, and Skipper Stephen sent out a Mayday call as the strong winds and heavy seas swept the vessel towards the sands. The harbour tug "Sea Griffon" sailed from Aberdeen at 5.30pm, and catching up with the "Ross Khartoum", three times passed lines to her, but on each occasion they parted before towing could begin. At 6.14pm the casualty took the ground off Balmedie, about 400 yards offshore, and shortly after 7.00pm the life-boat sailed, proceeding down wind and sea at full speed, as Coast Rescue Companies from Aberdeen, Belhelvie and Cruden Bay arrived on the storm-swept beach to set up their rocket equipment. As the "BP Forties" approached, her

The trawler ''Ross Khartoum'' ashore off Balmedie.

crew could see the trawler was being swept from stern to stem by enormous seas as she lay broadside on. It also became obvious that the stranded vessel had been washed over a seaward sandbank, before coming to rest on one further inshore. Given the life-boat's exposed rudders and propellors it would have invited disaster to approach any closer in those conditions of wind and tide. Slack water was due around 11.30pm that night, so after discussion with Skipper Stephen it was decided that he and his crew should remain on board until that time, when it was expected that conditions ought to improve somewhat. Equally, the efforts of the rescue parties to rig breeches buoy had failed as the ''Ross Khartoum'' was in the shallows and there was not enough height from the beach to effect a safe transfer.

The trawler's crew accordingly assembled in the wheelhouse and settled down to wait. The life-boat withdrew somewhat, patrolling slowly up and down some two cables to seaward and finding it very uncomfortable with the shallow water reflecting the full force of the storm. At around 10.00pm there was a change in the tempo of events with the casualty slowly driving to the northward as she was swept again and again. She also pivoted as she moved, always aground, until she stopped after having completed almost a full circle. Ten minutes later the

Coastguard requested a rescue helicopter from RAF Lossiemouth to evacuate the eight-man crew and Sea King ''Rescue 37'' took off at 10.43pm. Arriving on the scene at 11.30pm, and with the life-boat lying directly upwind to give the pilots a reference, it was not long before the seamen were being winched into the aircraft, two at a time. Records show that the last men were recovered at 12.11am, but not before one of them had stopped the generator to douse the lights! The life-boat was released to return to port, which she did by 1.00am, and almost simultaneously the big yellow Sea King landed at Dyce airport. However, the ''Ross Khartoum'' stayed on the beach, like the ''Sheriffmuir'', until 1984, when she was cut up for scrap.

''Ross Khartoum'' became a tourist attraction on Balmedie Beach before she was cut up for scrap in 1984.

1980-1985

Coxswain Albert Bird officially retired on 31 March, 1981 after 12 years' life-boat service, eight of them as Coxswain. He continues to be active in local RNLI affairs as Branch Public Relations Officer, giving talks and showing films describing the Institution's work, thus remaining an enthusiastic and valued member of the life-boat station's ''family''.

The year 1981 was quiet, with only two services. The first, whilst it could well have had very serious consequences, had its funny side. On 14 April, the ILB, whilst on exercise in the Bay, went to the assistance of a windsurfer in difficulties. The weather was fairly good, with only a slight swell close inshore, but as he approached the helmsman found himself a deal closer to the surfboard than was prudent. He accordingly swung the inflatable parallel to the

Albert and friends —
Coxswain A.W. Bird retires.

seas, but one came up under the boat, capsized it, and tossed its three-man crew into the water to join the somewhat bemused surfer. The life-boat was called out, but in the event was not required as the ILB, its occupants, and the windsurfer had been washed or waded ashore. When alerted, the author was at his weekly karate training session, and leaving hurriedly, reached the shed in white canvas suit and bare feet. This caused a deal of amusement amongst the crew when the incident had been resolved, and for a time there were suggestions that contact should be made with the Guiness Book of Records!

During 1982 the ''BP Forties'' was launched on six occasions, and spent a total of some 12¼ hours on service. On 17 February, two students were climbing on the Hareness Point cliffs near Cove, when 19-year old David Grant apparently became entangled and fell some 80 feet into the sea. His partner ran to raise the alarm, and in addition to the life-boat the Coastguard utilised the services of a small local craft. Search parties were soon scouring the area from the clifftops, and a Wessex helicopter from RAF Leuchars was also brought in.

Although the weather was fairly good, a moderate easterly wind had raised a choppy sea, and this, plus the many salmon nets in the area, made the task an exercise in concentration for the life-boat crew. Both the small boat and the helicopter proved ideal in searching the gullies and rocky shoreline, but it was not long before darkness put an end to the operation. A further sea search the following day had to be cancelled because of an overnight deterioration in the weather, and although the Coastguard checked the area from landward no trace of the young man was ever found.

There were just two calls for the life-boat during 1983, the second taking place during the night of Friday, 2 December. The city's police force was handling its usual range of minor incidents when it was reported that someone was in the sea just off Jay-Jay's nightspot on the Promenade. A patrol car was quickly at the locus and in the calm conditions a person could be seen swimming some 50 yards offshore. Constable Peter Bissett dived in after him, but the youth swam away, and the officer had to return to the shore whilst he could. By this time the rescue services had been alerted and as the life-boat's crew were making their hasty way to the station, the skipper of the inbound standby vessel ''Grampian Explorer'' offered the assistance of his fast rescue craft. This was gratefully accepted by the Roundhouse staff, and it was not long before the North Star vessel's crew had their craft in the water, to head shorewards where the youth's approximate line was marked by a flashing blue police car light. By this time the ''BP Forties'' was on her way to the scene at full speed, with her wash breaking clear over the

"B.P. Forties" on exercise.

Footdee quaysides as she passed. The life-boatmen had barely taken up lookout positions when the rigid inflatable rescue craft came out of the darkness, having picked up the swimmer on her very first sweep inshore. The unconscious 19-year old was taken on board the life-boat and treatment for hypothermia commenced as the "BP Forties" made all possible speed back to the pontoon berth at Blaikie's Quay and a waiting ambulance. On the following Monday the youth stood in the dock at Aberdeen Sheriff Court facing a charge of breach of the peace. Sentence was deferred until 23 December when he was placed on 12 months' probation.

Just over two weeks later, on Sunday 8 January, 1984, the BBC began the late-afternoon screening of a six-part TV documentary about the men and activities of the Humber Life-boat, the only RNLI station in which the crew members are all full-time employees. Aberdeen's crew had been looking forward to these programmes for some time, and there was accordingly an air of near-universal disbelief when, just as the titles were being screened, and Humber's 54-foot Arun "RNLI City of Bradford IV" was steaming across the screen, their "bleepers" went off.

(These items are now widely used for RNLI call-out purposes, and Aberdeen's are kindly provided by Seaforth Maritime Ltd, a large local shipping and oil-related company.) "It has to be a joke, and a poor one at that!", was the basic crew reaction as they sped harbourwards on icy roads. However, it had not been either a joke or an accidental transmission, for a small fishing vessel had been leaving the port when, very close to the shore, its engine had failed. An immediate distress message was transmitted, but the pilot cutter had been nearby and was soon able to put a line on board to tow the casualty to safety. By the time the life-boat crew had been stood down and returned to their homes it was inevitable that they had completely missed the documentary's first episode.

The evening of 26 January, 1984, was even by local winter conditions thoroughly unpleasant, with a full ESE gale blowing, and driving near-continuous sleet across the city. As the night wore on, the German-registered coaster "Darsser Ort", northbound with a cargo of drilling pipe, developed a 15 degrees list as the heavy casing broke loose and moved across the 700-ton vessel's hold. At this time the coaster was some 13 nautical miles SE of the port, and a call to the Coastguard soon resulted in the supply vessel "Cromarty Service" and the big tug "Euroman" proceeding to her assistance. At 10.35pm the life-boat was put on stand-by (this has the crew mustering and waiting on board with engines running, and ready for an immediate departure), and on his arrival Coxswain Norwan Trewren was told that the casualty had altered course towards the harbour and was attempting to reduce the list by pumping ballast across to the high side — a risky business in those conditions. However Captain Jurgen Schmidt considered this course to be less dangerous than to take his four-man crew and attempt to restow the cargo.

By 11.15pm the coaster was some six miles off Aberdeen, and her list had been reduced to seven degrees. Captain Atkinson, the Hon Secretary, had been assessing conditions on the bar, and with low water due around 1.00am, the Dee in full spate, and the gale, he reported a very unpleasant situation at the entrance. After a brief discussion it was decided that the life-boat should be launched before the bar became utterly impossible, and at 11.35pm the relief life-boat "Edith Emilie", a 52-foot Arun, slipped her moorings and proceeded across the tidal basin. As she passed Pocra Quay her crew battened everything down, taking even more thorough precautions than usual, and on entering the navigation channel it could be seen that the bar was an awesome sight even despite the winter darkness. Huge seas were breaking white across the entrance and its passage proved to be every bit as unpleasant as had been expected, with considerable motion being experienced once the relative shelter of Girdleness was passed. The radar was useless within a three-mile range due to the sea state so as course was shaped towards the estimated position of the "Darsser Ort", Captain Schmidt was asked to flash his ship's lights as a guide. It was about this time that the "Edith Emilie" took off from the top of a huge tidal lump of sea and crashed down into its trough. Later official estimates put the fall at over 20 feet, and no sooner had the life-boat shaken herself clear as she climbed into the next advancing crest, it broke and once again she dropped into the depths. This time the fall was even further, with crew members feeling as if they were space walking as she dropped. Following this second impact one of the life-boatmen indicated that he had hurt his foot, but from the others there was no immediate complaint.

Of more immediate interest was information on the casualty's intentions, and at this point her master contacted the life-boat to request advice on entering the port in such weather condi-

Aberdeen life-boatmen of the 1980's. Left to right: Bill Cowper, Iain Jack, George Walker, David Mitchell, Francis Cruickshank, John Corstorphine. Author on flying bridge.

tions. Information was duly passed on, but a rider was added that the safest thing to do would be to wait for daylight and the calmer conditions expected around high water. By this time the ''Edith Emilie'' had worked her way carefully round to take up a position off the coaster's starboard quarter, and the two vessels slowly proceeded northwards, rolling heavily as the huge seas came up astern of them (running before the sea is not one of the Arun's class's 'best points of sailing', and on this occasion keeping a heading proved heavy on arms and wrists). Captain Schmidt then decided for his own reasons to make an immediate run straight into the harbour, and once he had so advised the life-boat it dropped astern to await developments. The coaster drew ahead, turned to port, and passing the fairway buoy lined up the leading lights for his approach. A harbour pilot joined watchers in the Roundhouse to 'talk' the German into port. The seas sweeping across the entrance naturally pushed her towards the north pier, the graveyard of a number of ships in the past, and as Captain Schmidt told Coxswain Trewren later, ''I thought we had it. One sea came right across us and I could not see my ship forward of the bridge, just white water everywhere.''

The little coaster fought its way through the boiling surf, still listing to starboard, and then limped into the quieter waters of the harbour. Learning that the casualty was safely in port, the ''Edith Emilie'' followed, her drogue being streamed astern. The cabin door was tightly closed and the life-boat slowly approached the entrance, her engines just ticking over against the sea anchor's drag. Despite the storm, it was relatively quiet in the cabin, the life-boatmen very mindful that despite all their sophisticated modern equipment, their safe passage that night depended on a piece of equipment not out of place on one of Nelson's ships — that, plus some careful helm and engine movements to take care of the unexpected. In the event the elements seem to have relented somewhat as the transit of the navigation channel proved uneventful, and abeam of the Roundhouse the drogue was recovered. Now at a somewhat brisker pace the ''Edith Emilie'' hastened to her berth, and all was fast by 1.10am on 27th. As she was readied for sea again it was noted that the boathook was missing from its stowage forward, and that a section of spray chine had also been torn off. Equally, the crew had not escaped injury as, in addition to life-boatmen Jim Ferguson's broken foot (which together with ankle injuries later resulted in his premature retirement from the service), two others were hurt to the extent that they were off the active list for some six months. One other suffered cracked ribs, and minor bruising was a near-unanimous complaint. Despite this, most of them were at the annual Lifeboat Ball held that same evening, one of the most successful ever in the history of this major local social event — it has, admittedly to be recorded that few crew members were seen on the dance floor!

The "Edith Emilie" was quickly repaired, and exactly a fortnight later was again on service following a report of a small boat sinking north of the Donmouth. Despite a very thorough search in flat calm and hazy conditions, nothing was found and eventually the life-boat was stood down, the service being logged as a "false alarm with good intent".

Just over two months passed without further incident, but on 14 April, despite a strong offshore wind a local windsurfing instructor launched off the Beach into an ebb tide. As might be expected he soon found that he was unable to make his way back ashore, and luckily he just made fast on the outer edge of the last set of salmon nets before the Donmouth. His signals were eventually seen by a member of the public and as a result a Wessex helicopter from RAF Leuchars and the life-boat were both called out. The aircraft made good time in the strong wind, but as it crossed the Girdleness promontory, the "Edith Emilie" reached the scene. The shallow water and the proximity of the salmon nets made it foolhardy to approach the surfer in the big Arun-class boat, so her inflatable was launched and ran inshore. A few minutes later the casualty was on board, and taken out to the life-boat. The little inflatable then ran in again, and quickly returned with the surfboard, after which she followed the "Edith Emilie" back to port. The windsurfer was landed to a waiting ambulance at Pocra Quay, and once the "daughter boat" had been recovered, the life-boat returned to her station after a neat 50 minutes' service. Some three weeks later, on 8 May, 1984, the small lobster boat "A246", crewed by 47-year old Bill Mennie and 22-year old Dennis Cowe, was working its creels off Cove Bay when a breaking sea capsized the sturdy craft. It was early afternoon and both men were thrown into the water just offshore, to be approached, despite the risks, by another small boat. Dennis Cowe was able to grasp a thrown creel line and was pulled to safety, but the alarm was raised when there was no sign of his companion. The Inshore Life-boat was quickly launched, and was soon on its way across the moderate ground swell. To search the gullies and close-inshore areas the Coastguard brought in an RAF Sea King helicopter from Lossiemouth, and as the day wore on it was decided to call out the "BP Forties", not long back on station from a major refit. Other shore boats also joined in, and dodging amongst the swell and salmon nets, the whole area was scoured several times over, with the big Sea King backing deep into the gullies. It was eventually agreed that the missing man must be presumed lost and the life-boats were accordingly stood down to return to station where a local RNLI Branch Committee meeting had been taking place. Some six weeks later Mr Mennie's body was seen in the sea, and at the request of the police, the ILB was launched to recover it.

On Sunday, 29 July, 1984, the "BP Forties" and her crew were able to attend a quayside church service at Stonehaven to commemorate the RNLI's 160th anniversary. In her fresh paint, and dressed overall with signal flags, the life-boat made a fitting backdrop for the proceedings, and her crew were just returning for the passage back to Aberdeen when the Coastguard called to request her services. On board the 100,000 ton Sri Lankan-registered bulk carrier "Mega Star" a seaman had fallen down a ladder and injured his jaw. In perfect weather the life-boat left the little port, and it was not long before the huge shape of the bulk carrier loomed out of the haze. Tiny in comparison, the "BP Forties" went alongside the accommodation ladder, and the injured man was quickly taken to Aberdeen and a waiting ambulance.

The next two services contained an element of tragedy — early on the morning of 26 October a number of young people left a staff outing at Jay Jay's night spot. In high spirits they

The life-boat passes the South Breakwater on a calm day.

153

ran across the Beach Promenade, and started skylarking around as a long swell broke on the concrete in front of them. It was one of the year's biggest tides, and suddenly someone apparently slipped and fell. The next sea swept in, and more people were soon in the water, either washed in, or jumping in to help their friends. A horrified watcher called the police, and it was not long before Constable Malcolm Beverley was making a gallant effort to reach a figure seen floating offshore. His efforts were not in vain, but the pilot cutter picked up the body of another young girl from the edge of the surf. Called from their beds, the crew of the "BP Forties" raced to the station, and the life-boat reached the scene as shore parties kept a watch for further victims and tried to put together an account of the tragedy. Working on the very edge of the surf the life-boatmen searched the darkness, but all that was recovered were two ladies' handbags and a pocket diary, these being found off the North Pier. Saddened by the night's events, the life-boatmen returned to their homes after a two-hour service, but the next afternoon they were back at sea again.

This time the call followed a reported sighting by an Inverbervie man of what he thought was a hang glider crashing into the sea off the coast. As the rescue services swung into action, the "BP Forties" left her station and pounded southwards through the choppy sea. A long search then followed in company with a fast RGIT rescue craft from Stonehaven and an RAF Wessex helicopter from Leuchars, but nothing was found in the gathering darkness. By this time the Coastguard had ascertained that no local hang gliders or similar aircraft were missing, so the search was called off, and after a 3½ hour service, the lifeboat returned to her station. However, it soon became apparent that a microlight aircraft was missing, this on a flight from Kippen to Dundee with two persons on board. As a result the search was resumed for several days thereafter, but with local craft only as it was obvious that there could be no survivors.

Life-boatman Jim Ferguson
shows off the inshore
life-boat to interested
youngsters at an open day.

The Rocket Brigade

As part of the local agreement with the Institution, the RNLI agreed additionally to take over responsibility for the running of the port's secondary maritime rescue capability. This was comprised of rocket-propelled Life-saving apparatus (LSA), with two sets of equipment, one being based in Footdee, and the other on the Torry shore. In those pre-helicopter days, the LSA teams provided the only alternative source of rescue should life-boat be unable for any reason to approach a stranded vessel. The placing of the two units was totally logical as that in Footdee (where part of a building adjacent to the Roundhouse housed the cart with its rockets and lines) covered from the North Pier northwards, whilst that operating from a small stone structure close to the junction of St Fitticks and Greyhope Roads, took care of incidents to the southward. Dozens of somewhat similar units were located around the UK coastline, but the vast majority of these were run by HM Coastguard, and Aberdeen Harbour's LSA teams seem to have been unique in that they were run by the RNLI. Harbour staff and local volunteers turned out when required, often having to push their handcarts to the scene as neither appears ever to have been replaced by motor transport. Each was exercised on a quarterly basis, a degree of expectation being evident as the drills progressed to an actual heavy rocket firing. During the 37 years of the teams' existence, only a few calls seem to have been made upon their services, and these are detailed at the end of this book. In April, 1962, it was announced that the LSA facility would shortly be withdrawn from the port at the same time as the No. 2 (Beach) Life-boat, and the Footdee shed at least lay empty, with its gear mouldering and unused until 1968, when it was used to house the then-new Inshore Life-boat.

The Torry LSA in action — a
seaman comes ashore from
the trawler ''Spurs''.

Afterword

For sixty years now, the Royal National Life-boat Institution has operated the Life-boat Station at Aberdeen. The vessel on station in 1985 is a vastly different proposition from the first motor life-boat sent to the city in 1926 — different in design, in equipment and in power. Vastly different too, is the crew who man today's rescue craft. No longer is it sufficient for the Coxswain to run through the Squares of Footdee, kicking on doors and shouting, "Man the Life-boat!" — for today's crew hail from all over the city, from every walk of life, and are summoned to the boat by electronic "bleeper". The call however, which draws them from their firesides, their warm beds or their office desks, from patrolling their beat or tying up a ship in harbour, is still answered with the same urgency which motivated Tom Sinclair, George Flett and their crews in the early days — for the Aberdeen Life-boatmen of 1985 are still dedicated to the purpose of saving the lives of those in distress at sea, regardless of nationality or creed.

Life-boats and helicopters work closely together around the British coastline, with the Aberdeen station particularly involved.

ABERDEEN LIFE-BOAT STATION — RECORD OF R.N.L.I. SERVICES

No.	Date	Name of Casualty	Wind/ Weather	Duration	Lives Lost	Lives Saved	Brief Service Details	Life-boat
001	10/01/1926 11/01/1926	"STAR OF THE WAVE" of Aberdeen	Mod Gale/ Heavy Sea	7h 50m	1	None	Stranded Belhelvie Beach. Sailing L/boat unable to reach casualty.	WM. ROBERTS
002	27/07/1927	"VENETIA" of Aberdeen	SW Light/ Slight Sea	0h 55m	None	None	Stranded Girdleness in dense fog. Slid off and towed to port by tug "CHESTER".	EMMA CONSTANCE
003	06/09/1927	"BEN TORC" of Aberdeen	SE Mod Br/ Mod Sea	0h 57m	None	6	Stranded Gregness. Went alongside through rocks and took off 6 men.	EMMA CONSTANCE
004	25/02/1928 26/02/1928	"ISLE OF WIGHT" of Hull	SSW Md Br/ Mod Sea	4h 10m	None	None	Stranded Belhelvie beach. Eleven crew rescued by Newburgh L/boat.	EMMA CONSTANCE
005	18/03/1928	"AGNES H WEATHERLY"	SSW Mod Br/	4h 30m	None	None	Stranded 1nm N of Don mouth. Crew	EMMA CONSTANCE
006	22/06/1928	"REGAIN" of Lowestoft	Sw Strong Br/ Rough Sea	3h 50m	None	8	Stranded 1nm of Belhelvie CG Stn. Towed off by L/boat and escorted to Aberdeen.	EMMA CONSTANCE
007	25/10/1928	HM Drifter "LUNAR BOW"	SW Fresh Br/ Mod Sea	1h 23m	None	None	Stranded 800ft N of N Pier. Passed tow-line for tug. Stood by throughout.	EMMA CONSTANCE
008	25/10/1928	Ditto	Ditto Ditto	0h 55m	None	2	As above. Pulling L/boat landed one injured rating and one Midshipman.	ROBERT & ELLEN ROBSON
009	10/01/1929	"SHETLAND" of Leith	SE Mod Br/ Rough Sea	8h 35m	None	None	Requested assistance with 15ft water in hold. Flooding under control on arrival L/boat.	EMMA CONSTANCE
010	28/11/1929	"WILD ROSE" of Aberdeen	SE Strong Br/ Rough-Sea	5h 00m	None	None	Stranded Newtonhill on rocks. Nine crew landed by shore help.	EMMA CONSTANCE
011	22/01/1930	"JOHN G WATSON" of N Shields	SW Strong Br/ Rough Sea		None	None	Stranded 6½nm N of L/boat Hse. L/boat unable to approach casualty.	EMMA CONSTANCE
012	22/01/1930	Ditto	Ditto	7h 30m	None	10	As above. Pulling L/boat taken to scene by road, launched through surf, saved crew.	ROBERT & ELLEN ELLEN ROBSON
013	02/04/1930	"GLENCLOVA" of Aberdeen	SW Mod Br/ Heavy Br Sea	1h 30m	None	1	Stranded 300ft N of N Pier (broke moorings & drifted out of harbour). Pulling L/boat rescued one man.	ROBERT & ELLEN ROBSON
014	07/01/1931	"ST MERRYN" of Hull	W Light Br/ Smooth	0h 25m	None	None	Stranded Aberdeen Beach, and refloated without L/boat assistance.	EMMA CONSTANCE
015	09/04/1931	"RIGHTWAY" of N Shields	SW Mod Br/ Mod Sea/ Heavy Sea	3h 50m	None	None	Stranded ½nm S of Colliston CG Stn. Crew saved by LSA and cliff ladders.	EMMA CONSTANCE
016	02/06/1931	"LOYAL FRIEND" of Lowestoft	N Mod Br/ Mod Sea/ Heavy Surf	0h 35m	None	None	Collided with N Pier. L/boat alongside & stood by whilst LSA took off eleven crew.	EMMA CONSTANCE
017	11/06/1931	Unknown Vessel	SE Light Br/ Mod Sea	3h 0mm	None	None	SOS signals seen. Pulling L/boat towed to scene by tug "CHESTER". Nothing found.	ROBERT & ELLEN ROBSON
018	03/12/1931	"NAIRN" of Aberdeen	SE Whole Gale/ V Heavy Sea	4h 50m	None	None	Stranded 1nm S of Colliston. L/boat re-called prior to reaching scene.	EMMA CONSTANCE
019	14/08/1932	Whitehills Life-boat	Lt Airs/ Smooth	2h 30m	None	None	Broke down off Colliston. L/boat towed to Aberdeen	EMMA CONSTANCE
020	02/01/1933	"VENETIA" of Aberdeen	S Strong Gale/ V Heavy Sea	2h 30m	9	None	Stranded 3nm N of Stonehaven. All lost. Vessel total wreck. L/boat recalled.	EMMA CONSTANCE
021	18/01/1933	"BEN SCREEL" of Aberdeen	Var Lt Br/ Heavy Br Sea	3h 20m	None	None	Stranded Girdleness. Crew saved by LSA. L/boat unable to approach & stood by.	EMMA CONSTANCE
022	19/01/1933	"GENERAL BIRDWOOD" of Hull	N Mod Br/ Mod Sea	2h 40m	None	None	Close to Belhelvie CG Stn. Escorted vessel.	EMMA CONSTANCE
023	26/04/1933	False Alarm	S Fr Breeze Hy Sly Swell	1h 05m	None	None	L/boat recalled when passing Gregness.	EMMA CONSTANCE
024	03/07/1933	"CRETAN" of Glasgow	Calm/ Smooth		None	None	Towed off by pilot cutter after stranding L/boat not required.	
025	20/10/1933 21/10/1933	"FAIR ISLE" of Aberdeen	SE Fr Breeze/ Rough Sea	1h 10m	None	None	Broken rudder. Towed to Aberdeen by "BEN MEDIE" and escorted by L/boat.	EMMA CONSTANCE
026	23/10/1933 24/10/1933	"GRANERO" of Drammen	NE Mod Gale/ Rough Sea	18h 45m	None	7	Stranded Crawton Ness. L/boat took off part of crew, LSA the remainder.	EMMA CONSTANCE

Life-boatman Alan Charles looks on as a Bristow Tiger helicopter prepares for winching excercise.

No.	Date	Name of Casualty	Wind/ Weather	Duration	Lives Lost	Lives Saved	Brief Service Details	Life-boat
027	29/12/1933	"STRATHLEVEN" of Aberdeen	SE Mod Br/ V Hy Sea	3h 35m	None	None	Steering gear carried away off N Pier. Towed to berth by L/boat & then stood by whilst other fishing vessels entered port	EMMA CONSTANCE
028	17/01/1934	Gourdon & Stone-haven f/vessels.					L/boat crew on standy by only.	
029	20/12/1934	Unknown trawler	Var Lt/ Smooth Sea	1h 30m	None	None	Reported aground on the Ness Head. Nothing found after search.	EMMA CONSTANCE
030	14/02/1935	Various small local fishing yawls	N Mod Gale/ Rough Sea	4h 45m	None	None	Searched for vessels caught in gale. All entered port safely.	EMMA CONSTANCE
031	27/02/1935	"ELDORADO" of Aberdeen	SSE Mod Gale/ Heavy Sea	2h 50m	None	None	Stranded just N of Don mouth. Stood by until nine crew landed by LSA.	EMMA CONSTANCE
032	24/06/1935	"BALMORAL CASTLE" of Aberdeen	N Mod (Fog)/ Mod Sea	0h 40m	None	None	Stranded Greyhope Bay and refloated on rising tide.	EMMA CONSTANCE
033	27/09/1935	"EBOR ABBEY" of Aberdeen	WSW Mod Br/ Mod Sea	2h 35m	None	None	Stranded 2nm NE Belhelvie. L/boat recalled. (LSA and Newburgh L/boat attending).	EMMA CONSTANCE
034	05/11/1935	Yawls "PROCURE" & "QUEST" of Banff	SSE Mod Br/ Heavy Sea	1h 40m	None	None	Caught in gale. L/boat escorted to port.	EMMA CONSTANCE
035	25/12/1935	"GEORGE STROUD" of Aberdeen	SE Strong Br/ Heavy Sea	2h 28m	3	1	Grounded N Pier in Nav Channel. Lent assistance, took off one, but rest made no effort to board L/boat.	EMMA CONSTANCE
	* Bronze Medal Service (Coxswain Thos Sinclair)							
036	31/12/1935	"STRATHAIRLIE" of Aberdeen	Lt & Var Slt Swell		None	None	Broken rudder. L/boat recalled as passing pilot office.	EMMA CONSTANCE
037	17/01/1936	Aberdeen Pilot Cutter "WM PORTER"	ENE Fr Br/ Rough Sea	1h 20m	None	3	Cutter fouled propellor on wreck of "GEORGE STROUD" in Nav Channel. Three taken off by L/boat.	EMMA CONSTANCE
038	20/01/1936	Various fishing vessels	ESE Mod Gale/ Rough Sea		None	None	Stonehaven & Gourdon vessels. Stood by whilst they entered port.	EMMA CONSTANCE
039	06/02/1936	"PRETORIA" of Aberdeen	SW Mod Gale/ Rough Sea		None	None	Collision 6nm SE x S of Buchan Ness L/boat not required.	EMMA CONSTANCE
040	23/02/1936	"OCEAN GIFT" of Banff	ESE Str Gale/ V Hy Sea		None	None	Adrift in harbour. Crew assembly only.	
041	16/12/1936	"MARGARET & FRANCES" of Cockenzie	SSW Str Gale/ Vy Hy Sea	2h 35m	2	None	Stranded S of Belhelvie G Stn. L/boat launched on own initiative. Found vessel a wreck.	EMMA CONSTANCE
042	21/01/1937 22/01/1937	"STRATHEBRIE" of Aberdeen	SE Str Gale/ Vy Hy Sea	24h 40m	None	None	Requested help 50nm NE Aberdeen. L/boat search nothing found. Vessel towed to Buckie.	EMMA CONSTANCE
043	23/01/1937	"UTILITY" of Aberdeen	SE Str Gale/ Str Spate	1h 00m	None	None	Hung up by stern moorings. L/boat towed vessel to Fishmarket.	EMMA CONSTANCE
044	25/01/1937	Waterside Farm Sth Deeside Road	SE Gale/ Str Spate	3h 30m	None	3	Inhabitants marooned, pulling L/boat by road Launched into Dee for rescue.	ROBERT & ELLEN ROBSON
045	26/01/1937	"FAIRY" of Kings Lynn	SE Wh Gale/ Vy Hy Sea	4h 00m	None	None	Pulling L/boat on carriage to Belhelvie. Stood down on arrival No. 1 L/boat.	ROBERT & ELLEN ROBSON
046	Ditto	Ditto	Ditto Ditto	80h 07m	None	7	Ditto. Vessel under tow, but snapped & went ashore. L/boat rescued crew, proc Macduff due weather conditions.	EMMA CONSTANCE
	* (RNLI Silver Medal for Coxswain, 2 Bronze Medals for crew members).							
047	16/04/1937	"PAUL RYKENS" of Aberdeen	Calm/ Dense Fog	3h 00m	None	None	Stranded at Murcar, refloated own power.	EMMA CONSTANCE
048	13/08/1937	"STRATHAVON" of Scarborough	SE Breeze/ Fog, Mod Sea	4h 40m	None	None	Stranded Portlethen. L/boat ran out anchors, vessel refloated & escorted to Aberdeen.	J & W (RESERVE)
049	04/11/1937	"DELILA" of Aberdeen	S Fresh/ Sl Sea	10h 26m	None	None	Stranded 1nm S Belhelvie CG Stn, refloated with L/boat and tug assistance.	J & W (RESERVE)
050	04/11/1937	"ROSLIN" of Aberdeen	S Gale/ Vy Hy Brkg Sea	7h 10m	6	2	Stranded nr Ythan mouth. L/boat rescued 2 men from rigging, but damaged on service.	J & W (RESERVE)

(RNLI Silver Medal for Coxswain, 2 Bronze Medals for crew members).

Helicopter winching exercise
during the early seventies,
RNLB Ramsay Dyce.

No.	Date	Name of Casualty	Wind/ Weather	Duration	Lives Lost	Lives Saved	Brief Service Details	Life-boat
051	10/12/1937	Unknown vessel	ESE Str Br/ Hy Sea	4h 05m	None	None	L/boat launched by CG, no trace despite thorough search.	J & W (RESERVE)
052	30/12/1937	"CALVINIA" of Aberdeen	NWN Mod Br	3h 50m	None	None	Lost prop, L/boat searched, no trace, vessel had been towed to Abdn by "INVERFORTH".	EMMA CONSTANCE
053	15/01/1938	"P FANNON" of Aberdeen					Crew assy only — vessel towed into Abdn by "STURDEE"	
054	16/02/1938	"SAXON (Yawl) of Aberdeen	NE Fr Br/ Rough Sea	1h 35m	None	3	Disabled in Greyhope Bay & towed in by pilot cutter	
055	25/08/1938	"CARRY ON" of Aberdeen	Vrble, Fog/ Slt Swell	1h 25m	None	None	Aground on Girdlestone, towed off by L/boat.	EMMA CONSTANCE
056	04/12/1938	"BRANCH" (Yawl) of Montrose	S Mod Gale/ Rough Sea	3h 20m	None	None	Rep in diffy off Findon, L/boat searched nothing found. Vessel made Stonehaven.	EMMA CONSTANCE
057	22/01/1939	Unknown Yawl	ESE Sl Br/ Sl Sea	2h 05m	None	None	Rep capsized off Br of Don, searched, nothing found.	EMMA CONSTANCE
058	15/09/1939	Rep torpedoed steamer	NE Mod Br Mod Sea	2h 10m	None	None	Proc at full speed to scene, told not reqd, returned to port.	EMMA CONSTANCE
059	04/10/1939 05/10/1939	"STROMNESS" of Aberdeen	SE Gale/ Hy surf	5h 15m	None	None	Stranded off Broad Hill, crew landed LSA L/boat oars fouled rkt lines, stern grounded.	ROBERT & ELLEN ROBSON
060	10/10/1939	"SOLSTAD" of Oslo	SE Storm/ Hy Sea	7h 30m	None	None	Steering gear damage, coal shortage. Searched, nothing found, vessel had been towed to Leith.	EMMA CONSTANCE
061	31/10/1939	"CAIRNMONA" of Newcastle	E/ly Mod/ Rough Sea	9h 30m	None	None	Torpedoed off Rattray Hd by U-13. Other vessel landed survivors P/head.	EMMA CONSTANCE
062	12/12/1939	"CIMBRIA" of Copenhagen					Sranded nr Stonehaven. Assembly only.	
063	18/12/1939 19/12/1939	"TRINITY NB" of Granton	WSW x 2/ Mod Sea	19h 55m	Unknown	None	Rept. bombed by enemy a/craft 80nm ENE Aberdeen. Searched — no trace.	EMMA CONSTANCE
064	09/01/1940	"GOWRIE" of Dundee			Unknown	None	Sunk by enemy action 5nm SxE Newtonhill Wreckage only found. Bombed.	
065	09/01/1940	"FEDDY" of Copenhagen	SSW Fresh/	7h 20m	Unknown	2	2nm off G/ness. Bombed & on fire on tow to Aberdeen. Some crew taken off. Reports very confused these incidents.	EMMA CONSTANCE
066	09/01/1940	"IVAN KONDRUP" of Copenhagen						
067	10/01/1940	"FEDDY" (see above)	SSW Lt/	9h 30m	None	None	Towing to Aberdeen with L/boat as escort	EMMA CONSTANCE
068	09/02/1940	"LILY" of Aberdeen	SW x 3/ Mod Swell	1h 40m	None	3	Disabled 1½nm Br of Don. Located and towed into Aberdeen by L/boat.	EMMA CONSTANCE
069	06/03/1940	Bombed vessel	NW Mod/ Sl Sea	2h 25m	None	None	Searched, but found nothing	EMMA CONSTANCE
070	16/07/1940	Unknown vessel	Vrb Airs/ Sl Sea	2h 00m	None	None	Searched, but no trace.	GEORGE & ELIZABETH GOW
071	18/07/1940	Convoy bombed					6nm 063° Br of Don. Stand by at station for 2h 30m.	
072	20/10/1940	"CONAKRIAN" of Freetown	ESE x 5-6/ Choppy? Rough	7h 40m	Unknown	None	Torpedoed 9nm 130° G/ness. Tug towed vessel to Aberdeen with L/boat escorting.	EMMA CONSTANCE
073	21/10/1940	"CONAKRIAN" of Freetown	Squalls 5-7/ Hy Sea	1h 33m	None	2	Anchored Aberdeen Bay in heavy weather. L/boat took off RN offr & signalman.	EMMA CONSTANCE
074	23/10/1940	"CONAKRIAN" of Freetown	Mod E Gale/ Mod Sea	1h 12m	None	23	Took off 23 men at request of RN authorities.	EMMA CONSTANCE
075	03/04/1941	"CAIRNIE" of Methil	ESE x 7-8/ Vy Hy Sea	1h 54m	None	7	In distress harbour entrance after being bombed earlier. Steering damaged, grounded.	EMMA CONSTANCE
077	24/07/1941	Unknown vessel	Calm/ Smooth Sea	1h 11m			Vessel reported ashore, but life-boat recalled as coast search found nothing.	EMMA CONSTANCE
078	13/08/1941	Unknown vessel					Standby at station only.	

Francis Cruickshank —
Life-boatman.

No.	Date	Name of Casualty	Wind/Weather	Duration	Lives Lost	Lives Saved	Brief Service Details	Life-boat
079	02/10/1941	British aircraft	W x 4/ Mod Sea	1h 30m	None	None	L/boat recalled after pilot rescued by other agency.	EMMA CONSTANCE
080	13/03/1942	Unknown vessel	SSW x 6/ Hy Sea	0h 50m	Unknown	None	No report filed.	EMMA CONSTANCE
081	15/03/1942	HMS ''HYDERABAD'' & ''BRUNO'' (Tug)	S x 3-4/ Smooth Sea	4h 30m	None	None	HM ship grounded in Nav Channel & tug also grounded. L/boat towed off tug which then hit L/boat. Corvette refloated herself.	EMMA CONSTANCE
082	14/04/1942	''BON ACCORD'' of Aberdeen					No report available.	
083	02/04/1943	Unknown vessels					No report available	
084	07/04/1945	Schooner ''ELSE'' of Thisted	N x 6-9/ Vy Rough Sea	0h 40m	None	None	In difficulties off S B/water. Vessel towed into port, with L/boat escorting.	EMMA CONSTANCE
085	29/11/1943	''TREVORIAN'' of St Ives	Lt W'ly Airs/ Smooth Sea	3h 41m	None		No detailed report available	EMMA CONSTANCE
086	23/10/1944	''KEILEHAVEN'' of Rotterdam	SE x 3-4/ Long Gr Swell	4h 45m	None (*t/ferred)	40*	110° 6nm Br of Don, abandoned. Men taken off by US ship. L/boat put 12 back on board, landed rest.	EMMA CONSTANCE
087	10/04/1945 11/04/1945	Smack ''ALBERT VICTOR'' of Vaag, Faeroes	E x 3-4/ Brkg Surf	3h 30m	None	9	Stranded on Beach whilst adj compasses. Tug unable refloat. L/boat took off crew & pilots.	EMMA CONSTANCE
088	13/04/1945	''MARIA'' of Ymuiden	Lt E'ly Mod Sea	6h 00m	None	None	Stranded Abdn. beach. Kedged self off with L/boat standing by throughout.	EMMA CONSTANCE
089	22/05/1945	HM MTB 2007	NE Mod/ Br Surf	4h 50m	None	20	Stranded 150yds E of old S B/water. Attempt to tow failed. 20 off by L/boat, 1 by LSA.	JOHN RUSSELL
090	30/07/1945	''MAY LILY'' of Peterhead	Lt Airs/ Sl Sea	2h 40m	None	None	Engine failure on passage. Big air/sea search but made P/head under own power.	EMMA CONSTANCE
091	19/10/1945	HM MFV 1172	SSE x 3-5/ Mod/Rough Sea	1h 49m	None	5	Disabled 112° 3nm Gregness. L/boat towed vessel to Aberdeen.	EMMA CONSTANCE
092	19/12/1945	''T L DEVLIN'' of Granton	S x 5-7/ Hy Sea	8h 25m	None	None	Leaking 22nm SE of Aberdeen. L/boat escorted vessel to port.	EMMA CONSTANCE
093	21/12/1945	''SPARKLING STAR'' of Peterhead	Lt S'ly Airs/ Smooth Sea	4h 02m	None	None	Fouled propeller off Belhelvie. Self able to clear, L/boat not required.	EMMA CONSTANCE
094	20/01/1946	''SPURS'' of Grimsby			None	None	Aground in Nav Channel. L/boat damaged whilst standing by. Tug also aground.	EMMA CONSTANCE
095	07/08/1946	''HARMONIOUS II'' of Aberdeen	SW x 2-3/ Lt/Mod Sea	4h 30m	None	6	Broke down off Collieston and towed to port by L/boat.	EMMA CONSTANCE
096	20/10/1947	''HARVEST GLEANER'' of Buckie	SSE x 5/ Mod Sea	5h 30m	None	None	Towed into Aberdeen by other vessel — L/boat recalled.	EMMA CONSTANCE
097	05/02/1948	''NORTHMAN'' of Aberdeen	S x 4-6/ Hy Br Surf	78h 10m	None	None	2nm S of Belhelvie — stranded. L/boat also grounded & refloated by tug.	EMMA CONSTANCE
098	13/01/1949	''WELBECK'' of Grimsby	SW x 2/ Sm/Sl Sea	2h 28m	None	None	Stranded 4 cbls N of N Pier. L/boat passed tow for tug, and escorted. No. 2 L/boat on s/by.	EMMA CONSTANCE
099	23/09/1949	''ALIRMAY'' of Aberdeen	SE x 3-4/ Mod/Hy Sea	0h 40m	None	None	Stranded Downies, P/lethen. L/boat not req'd & recalled to station.	EMMA CONSTANCE
100	24/09/1949	''BRIGHTSIDE'' of Dundee	E x 1-2/ Sl Sea	3h 20m	None	None	Stranded 5 cbls S Collieston. Crew landed by drifter. L/boat not required.	EMMA CONSTANCE
101	17/09/1950	''SAGA'' of Aberdeen	SSE x 8-9/ Vy High Sea	6h 30m	None	None	Engine failure. L/boat recalled, but see below.	EMMA CONSTANCE
102	17/09/1950	Ditto	SSE x 8/9 Vy High Sea	8h 00m	None	None	Engine failure 2 1/2nm abeam Collieston. Towed to P/head by P/head L/boat. Abdn L/boat escorted.	EMMA CONSTANCE
103	26/09/1950	''LYNDBURN'' of Aberdeen	NE x 4/ Rough Hy Swell	1h 00m	None	1	Grounded Nav Channel. Tugs attempted, but unable to refloat. L/boat took off one man.	EMMA CONSTANCE

Three long-serving
Aberdeen Life-boatmen.
Left to right: second
mechanic George Walker,
second coxswain William
Cowper, crewman Francis
Cruickshank.

No.	Date	Name of Casualty	Wind/ Weather	Duration	Lives Lost	Lives Saved	Brief Service Details	Life-boat
104	14/02/1951	Yauwl "GLEN" of Aberdeen	SE x 3-4/ Slight Sea	1h 10m	None	2	Broken down 1nm ENE of Gregness. L/boat towed to Aberdeen.	EMMA CONSTANCE
105	06/11/1951	Caravan encampment River Dee	SE x 7-9/ River in spate	17h 45m	None	31	Caravans marooned by floods. Beach L/boat & carriage to Mill Inn. Engine fouled. Salmon coble brought and used in place.	GEORGE & ELIZABETH GOW
106	07/01/1952	Various small fishing vessels	SSW x 3/ Choppy Sea	3h 40m	None	None	Reported in difficulties. Searched — all accounted for.	HILTON BRIGGS
107	18/08/1952	RAF Aircraft (Vampire)	NE x 4-5/ Choppy Sea	13h 45m	2	None	Crashed 20nm SE of Girdleness. Searched but no trace. Aircraft from Leuchars.	HILTON BRIGGS
108	23/08/1952	"LOCH LOMOND" of Aberdeen	SSW x 5/ Hy Br Sea	1h 00m	None	None	Aground S side of N Pier in Nav Channel. Crew taken off by LSA with L/boat standing by.	HILTON BRIGGS
109	09/02/1953	"MARY GOWANS" & "TRUSTFUL III" of Aberdeen	SW x 2/ Hy Br Swell	0h 55m	None	None	Required assistance to enter. Advice given & stood by as heavy swell at port entrance.	HILTON BRIGGS
110	12/02/1953	"GENERAL BOTHA" of Aberdeen	NNE x 5-6/ Hy Br Sea	1h 25m	None	None	Short of food but port closed. Supplies taken off and put aboard.	HILTON BRIGGS
111	16/09/1953	RN Aircraft from RNAS Arbroath	SSE x 3-4/ Mod Sea				Reported crashed off Tod Head. Stood by at station. A/craft found inland.	HILTON BRIGGS
112	26/10/1953	"TRUSTFUL III" of Aberdeen	SSE x 8-9/ Hy Conf Sea	6h 35m	None	4	Fouled propellor 1½nm SE of Muchalls. Towed off lee shore and with great difficulty to port.	HILTON BRIGGS
113	24/01/1954	"POSEIDON" of Aberdeen	SSE x 8/ Hy Conf Sea	5h 25m	None	4	Engine breakdown 2nm ExS of Tod Head. Assisted Montrose L/boat and towed to Aberdeen.	HILTON BRIGGS
114	04/06/1955	"MARIA" of Scheveningen	E x 5-6/ Rough Sea	5h 35m	None	None	"MARIA" towing "DOLPHIN", which sank. Doctor req'd for survivors. Taken out by L/boat.	HILTON BRIGGS
115	09/07/1955	Unknown motor boat	Variable/ Smooth Sea	4h 06m	None	None	Reported upturned boat ½nm off Muchalls Searched, but no trace.	J W ARCHER (RESERVE)
116	06/08/1955	"WESTWARD HO" of Aberdeen	NW x 4/ Mod/Rough Sea	5h 15m	None	4	Engine breakdown 3nm S of Findon Ness. L/boat towed to Stonehaven.	J W ARCHER (RESERVE)
117	20/10/1955	"STURDEE" of Aberdeen	S x 4-5/ Hy Br Sea	1h 25m	None	11	Stranded ¼nm N of Beach Ballroom. L/boat took off 11 men in 4 runs alongside. (No 2 boat on s/by).	HILTON BRIGGS
118	30/01/1956	"YORK CITY" of Grimsby "JUNELLA" of Hull	SSW x 5-6/ Hy Range	1h 40m	None	None	Gave advice and stood by whilst entered port. Bar breaking heavily in spate.	HILTON BRIGGS
119	09/02/1956	"MORMACOAK" of New York	SSE x 2-4/	2h 00m	None	None	Took doctor to vessel off Girdleness.	HILTON BRIGGS
120	18/03/1956	"KRYMOV" of USSR	SSE x 5-6/ Mod/Hy Br Swell	2h 55m	None	None	Stranded 2nm N of Bridge of Don. Offered help, but no response and assistance refused.	HILTON BRIGGS
121	23/05/1956	"RENNYHILL" of Aberdeen	Var Airs/ Lt/Mod Sea	5h 30m	None	10	Stranded S side of S B/water root. Brought to port by L/boat.	HILTON BRIGGS
122	16/08/1956 17/08/1956	RN Cutter	Lt SW Airs/ Calm	0h 55m	None	5	Overdue. Found 2nm E of Aberdeen becalmed. Towed to port by L/boat	JJ & SW (RESERVE)
123	03/11/1956	Unknown	N x 3-4/ Mod Sea	3h 40m	None	None	Reported overturned dinghy. Search, nothing found.	HILTON BRIGGS
124	06/11/1956	Vampire A/craft					Engine failure. Force-landed on beach. Crew assembly only. (612 Sqdn Vampire)	
125	08/11/1956	"STEPHENS" of Fraserburgh					Ashore 2nm S of Collieston. P/head L/boat attended. Crew assembly only.	
126	09/11/1956	"SOLSKIN" of Oslo	SE x 6/ Hy Sea & Swell	9h 01m	None	16	20° list & leaking badly. L/boat escorted to port (10nm E of Tod Head).	HILTON BRIGGS
127	26/11/1956 27/11/1956	"STRINDHEIM" of Trondheim	NW x 9/ Vy Hy Conf Sea	13h 25m	None	None	47nm 065° Aberdeen, 13° list, 6ft water in hold. L/boat escorted to port.	HILTON BRIGGS
128	29/12/1956	"LOMBARD" of Grimsby	S x 3/ Heavy Sea	4h 25m	None	None	Ashore Cruden Skares. L/boat came in on drogue. Touched sandbank. 2 crew injured.	HILTON BRIGGS
129	01/03/1957	"FERM" of Kristinehamn (Sweden)					Crew assembly only. Newburgh life-boat used. Vessel aground of Ythan mouth.	

"B.P. Forties" and friends.
Helicopter exercise with
Bristow S-61 aircraft, 1977.

No.	Date	Name of Casualty	Wind/ Weather	Duration	Lives Lost	Lives Saved	Brief Service Details	Life-boat
130	29/09/1957	"OUR MERIT" of Lowestoft	N x 7-8/ Vy Rough Sea	3h 45m	None	None	Vessel reported sinking 35/40nm SE Aberdeen. L/boat recalled. Sank under tow oft S/haven	HILTON BRIGGS
131	25/12/1957 26/12/1957	"AMOS" of Copenhagen	SW x 7/ Vy Hy Conf Sea	21h 55m	None	1	Medical assistance. One man landed in heavy weather.	HILTON BRIGGS
132	21/01/1958	"LUFFNESS" of Granton	W x 2-3/ Sl Sea	0h 55m	None	None	Grounded N Pier. Crew taken off by pilot cutter. L/boat attempted to run moorings.	HILTON BRIGGS
133	08/05/1958	"STEERSMAN" of London	SSE x 4/ Gr Swell	3h 42m	None	None	Stranded Balmedie. L/boat informed by casualty no danger. Stood down.	HILTON BRIGGS
134	29/07/1958	Caravan Encampment River Dee (Mill Inn)	NNW x 4	4h 45m	None	14	Marooned due to flooding of river.	Salmon Coble.
135	10/08/1958	"OCEAN STARLIGHT" of Gt Yarmouth	S x 1 (Fog) Calm				Aground Girdleness. Crew assembly only.	
136	18/01/1959	Unknown vessel	SW x 2-3/ Lt Swell	2h 10m	None	None	Reported red flares off Br of Don. Search — nothing found.	RAMSAY DYCE
137	25/03/1959	"CADORNA" of Aberdeen	S x 2 fog/ Hy SE Swell	6h 40m	None	None	Engine defects 3nm NE Aberdeen in thick fog Search — no trace. Towed to Aberdeen.	RAMSAY DYCE
138	27/06/1959	"HUIBERDINA GIJSBERTHA" (DUTCH)	Var x 2 fog/ Calm	2h 30m	None	None	Stranded in dense fog 3nm ENE Aberdee. Refloated by herself, towed Abdn by tug.	J M MCPHEE (RESERVE)
139	17/10/1959	"CROWN" of Aberdeen	SE x 6/ Mod Sea				Stand by only as vessel sailed against Round House advice.	
140	28/10/1959	"DAVID OGILVIE" of Aberdeen	NNE x 8/ Hy Br Sea	1h 20m	None	1	Broke moorings & grounded S side of Nav Channel. Took off watchman (sleeping).	RAMSAY DYCE
141	18/11/1959	"BEN EARN" of North Shields	SE x 9				Assembly only — 2h 30m	
142	19/01/1960	Seine Netters	SE x 6				Assembly only — 2h 00m	
143	14/05/1960	Pilot Cutter No 1 of Aberdeen	ESE x 3-4/ Mod Swell	0h 20m	None	None	Stranded S B/Water. Sole occupant swam ashore Vessel total loss.	RAMSAY DYCE
144	12/07/1960	Yacht "HELEN KERR"	NW x 2/ Smooth Sea	0h 35m	None	None	Taken in tow by other vessel. L/boat recalled in Channel.	RAMSAY DYCE
145	12/04/1961 13/04/1961	"CONTENDER" of Granton	SW x 5/ Mod Sea	4h 20m	None	None	Stranded 2-3nm S of Cruden Skares. Crew ashore by raft. L/boat stood by.	RAMSAY DYCE
* First service Coxswain Leo Clegg DSC.								
146	09/12/1961	"FRUITFUL BOUGH" of Peterhead	SSW x 4-5/ Mod/Hy Br Surf	2h 20m	None	None	Stranded 5nm N of Aberdeen. Crew waded ashore. L/boat stood by.	RAMSAY DYCE
147	04/05/1962	Man over cliffs	SSE x 1-2/ Slight Sea	2h 08m	1	None	Incident ocurred at Cove. Search called off.	RAMSAY DYCE
148	26/05/1962	Man washed off rocks	NNE x 6-8/ Mod Sea	2h 28m	1	None	Ditto	RAMSAY DYCE
149	04/07/1962 05/07/1962	"MAG" of Peterhead	NNW x 5/ Mod Sea	3h 05m	None	3	Fouled propellor 4nm ESE Girdleness. L/boat towed to port.	W & S (RESERVE)
150	14/11/1962 15/11/1962	"POULANN" of Esbjerg	NW x 6-7/ Hy Gr Swell	14h 26m	None	None	Skipper reported injured N61E of Aberdeen. (Lady) doctor taken out.	RAMSAY DYCE
151	19/05/1963	"RNLB NORMAN NAISMITH" (ON.836)	N x 2-3/ Slight Sea	6h 30m	None	5	Engine trouble. L/boat towed casualty to Newburgh.	THOMAS MCCUNN (RESERVE)
152	22/09/1963	"WINAWAY" of Fraserburgh	SW x 2/ Lt S'ly Sea	2h 35m	None	None	Engine b/down 8nm E S/haven. L/boat fouled own prop, casualty towed to S/haven by MFV.	RAMSAY DYCE
153	20/11/1963	Military Aircraft	W x 2/ Sl Sea	4h 00m	None	None	Believed to have come down in sea 6-8nm of G/ness. Searched but no trace.	RAMSAY DYCE
154	24/11/1963	"ASTON VILLA" of Grimsby	SW x 3-4/ Sl/Mod Sea	0h 38m	None	None	E/room flooding 2nm NNE Aberdeen. L/boat escorted to Aberdeen. (20 aboard).	RAMSAY DYCE
155	17/02/1964	Coble ME 151 of Montrose	N x E R & Conf Sea	2h 10m	None	6	Engine failure off Altens, 50 yds from rocks Crew on board L/boat and towed to Aberdeen.	RAMSAY DYCE
156	01/03/1964	"BAYWYKE" of Whitby.	SSW x 3/ Choppy Sea	4h 00m	None	4	Lost — faulty compass. Found and escorted to port by L/boat. (Used red flares).	RAMSAY DYCE

Second Mechanic George
Walker.

No.	Date	Name of Casualty	Wind/ Weather	Duration	Lives Lost	Lives Saved	Brief Service Details	Life-boat
157	10/03/1964	"ANNIE RITCHIE" of Fraserburgh	NE x 3/ Smooth Sea	3h 30m	None	2	Engine failure — 3-4nm E x N of Belhelview CG Stn. L/boat towed to Aberdeen.	RAMSAY DYCE
158	30/04/1964	"ABILITY" of Kirkcaldy	SW x 1-2/ Smooth Sea	1h 33m	None	None	Stranded Girdleness. L/boat rope refused and refloated herself. L/boat esc. to Aberdeen.	RAMSAY DYCE
159	04/07/1964	Small rowing boat	W x 1/ Slight Sea	1h 06m	None	2	Two boys incapable of handling boat 1/2nm off G/ness. Taken on board L/boat & towed to Abdn.	RAMSAY DYCE
160	14/07/1964	"SIRIUS" of Buckie	SW x 3-4 Rough Sea	24h 53m	4	None	Collision with Polish trawler "ZIEBA" N89E 91nm Aberdeen. Search but no trace.	RAMSAY DYCE
161	29/07/1964	Unknown	NNW x 3/ Smooth Sea	4h 28m	None	None	Red flares reported off Cruden Skares. E German ship in area, but no commn.	RAMSAY DYCE
162	04/08/1964	Open boat "SEAHAWK" of Aberdeen	SW x 2/ Smooth	1h 50m	None	3	Red flares reported 2nm SxE G/ness. Three men taken on board L/boat & towed to Aberdeen.	GEORGE & SARAH STRACHAN (RESERVE)
163	22/09/1964	"MARGARET II" of Aberdeen (Yawl)	WSW x 3-4/ Smooth	2h 35m	None	3	Red flares reported 3nm, N25E Gregness. Taken in tow by L/boat to Aberdeen.	RAMSAY DYCE
164	13/01/1965	"JUBILEE" of Aberdeen.	SE x 4-6/ Rough	2h 11m	None	None	Broke down off Belhelvie, but repaired Escorted to Aberdeen by L/boat.	RAMSAY DYCE
165	02/04/1965	"DINEIDDWG" of Aberdeen	SW x 1-2/ Slight Sea	1h 36m	None	7	Aground Girdleness in thick fog. Towed off by L/boat.	RAMSAY DYCE
166	04/09/1965	Man & two boys swept off rocks	NNE x 5/ Vy Rough Sea	3h 35m	3	None	Searched area S of Gregness. No trace.	RAMSAY DYCE
167	25/10/1965	RN Aircraft from RNAS Lossiemouth	SE x 2/ Slight Sea	1h 45m	None	None	Crashed into sea off Slains Castle after mid air collision (Hunter) Helo rescued pilot.	RAMSAY DYCE
168	18/11/1965	Unknown	E x 5/ Rough Sea	3h 20m	None	None	Flares reported by CG l/nm N of Br of Don CG Stn Search, no trace — poss a/c on exercise.	RAMSAY DYCE
169	02/02/1966	"ROSS FORTUNE" of Grimsby	E x 5/ Vy Rough Sea	3h 46m	None	10	Broken down & drifting ashore in Abdn Bay. L/boat passed line to tug which towed to Abdn.	RAMSAY DYCE
170	01/04/1966	"BRAKE I" of Brake, Germany	WNW x 3-5	3h 10m	None	None	Engine room leak. Other vessels in area. L/boat recalled.	RAMSAY DYCE
171	28/05/1966	Boy over cliffs at Cove	WNW x 3-4/ Smooth	0h 28m	1	None	Body recovered by shore party whilst L/boat en route — recalled.	RAMSAY DYCE
172	23/07/1966	Rowing boat "DAFFODIL"	SW x 2/ Slight Sea	0h 40m	None	None	Reported in difficulties off Findon GC Stn. Rescued by other vessel, L/boat recalled.	RAMSAY DYCE
173	12/12/1966	"HEIKENDORFF" of Kiel	SE x 6-8/ Vy Rough Sea	3h 40m	None	None	Required medical help. Port closed, but doctor taken out & put on board (injured) with diff.	RAMSAY DYCE
174	16/12/1966	"SEMNOS II" of Aberdeen	W x 3/ Rough Sea	5h 15m	None	None	Stranded R Ythan mouth. Crew off by LSA & L/boat unable to close due shallows & hy seas.	RAMSAY DYCE
175	08/02/1967	Unknown	NW x 2/	3h 31m	None	None	Red flares reported off Newtonhill. Assumed hoax & L/boat recalled.	RAMSAY DYCE
176	18/02/1967	"CRYSTAL RIVER" of Fraserburgh.	NW x 2/ Mod Sea	2h 35m	None	4	Broken down Abdn Bay N of G/ness Lt Ho. Towed with diffy by L/boat to Abdn.	RAMSAY DYCE
177	20/06/1967	Army Canoes	W x 5/ Mod Sea	7h 35m	2	None	Capsized on trng ex N of Br of Don L/boat & military recovered canoes.	RAMSAY DYCE
178	21/06/1967	Ditto	SW x 1-2/ Slight Sea	4h 35m	1	None	One body located by RAF Shackleton & recovered by L/boat.	RAMSAY DYCE
179	28/06/1967	Yacht "BLOW ME" of Aberdeen	SSW x 2/ Smooth Sea	5h 15m	None	None	Lack of coastal knowledge — towed into port by pilot cutter.	RAMSAY DYCE
180	06/08/1967	Rubber dinghy	SSW x 2-3/	4h 55m	None	None	Reported adrift off Murcar. Search with help but nothing found & recalled.	RAMSAY DYCE
181	03/01/1968	Rubber Dinghy	W x 2/ Smooth Sea	74h 33m	None	4	Dinghy overdue. Found after search by L/boat	SOUTHERN AFRICA (RESERVE)

The author — Coxswain
N.D.L. Trewren.

No.	Date	Name of Casualty	Wind/ Weather	Duration	Lives Lost	Lives Saved	Brief Service Details	Life-boat
182	11/05/1968	Cliff rescue	NW x 4/ Slight		1		Muster only. Body recovered by cliff party.	
183	24/06/1968	"FLOWER" of Buckie	WNW x 3-4/	5h 55m	None	None	Sank. Crew on rafts and picked up by "WALNUT"	RAMSAY DYCE
184	02/08/1968	Missing 3-year old girl	E x 2/ Smooth	0h 50m	None	None	Missing on beach at Br of Don, but found ashore.	RAMSAY DYCE
185	04/08/1968	Object in water	S x l/ Smooth	1h 34m	None	None	Sighted 2nm 163° of Collieston. Helicopter checked — no casualty.	RAMSAY DYCE
186	12/10/1968 13/10/1968	"SEMNOS II" of Aberdeen	SW x 8/ Vy Rough Sea	9h 10m	None	7	Engine failure 086° Belhelvie 4nm. Tow parted and taken by L/boat in tow to Peterhead.	RAMSAY DYCE
187	05/11/1968	Unknown	SSE x 4/ Mod Sea	9h 00m	None	None	Report of flare 43nm E of port. L/boat searched but no trace.	RAMSAY DYCE
188	19/03/1969	Various Vessels	SE x 5-6/ Mod	4h 15m	None	None	Stood by after port re-opened following prolonged ESE gales	SOUTHERN AFRICA (RESERVE)
189	14/04/1969	Man over cliffs	SW x 3-4/ Mod Sea	2h 55m	1	None	Man over cliffs at Portlethen. L/boat searched & grappled, but no trace.	SOUTHERN AFRICA (RESERVE)
190	19/04/1969	"FIONA" of Brixham	N x 3/ Mod Sea	2h 45m	None	None	Engine failed 1½nm off Portlethen. No flares. Rescued by fishermen. L/boat towed to port.	SOUTHERN AFRICA (RESERVE)
191	26/09/1969	"DEWY ROSE"		1h 52m	None	None	Engine failed. Stonehaven ILB towed to that port.	RAMSAY DYCE
192	12/12/1969	"STAR OF BETHLEHEM"					Rescued by Stonehaven vessel.	RAMSAY DYCE
193	04/02/1970	"ALDEBARAN" of E Germany	N x 3-4/ Choppy Sea	1h 25m	None	None	Reported man overboard 45nm E of Aberdeen but found by other vessels & L/boat recalled.	RAMSAY DYCE
194	09/03/1970	"RUSHING WATER" of Johnshaven	N x 3/ Smooth Sea	1h 27m	None	None	Engine failure, but repaired and continued passage. L/boat recalled.	RAMSAY DYCE
195	06/05/1970	"SUMMERSIDE" of Leith	SE x 5/ Rough Sea	9h 57m	None	None	Aground N of Carron Point Stonehaven. Crew rescued by LSA.	RAMSAY DYCE
196	14/07/1970	Unknown	NNE x 6-8/ Rough Sea	2h 15m	None	None	Report of small boat capsizing off Beach Ballroom. Search but nothing found.	RAMSAY DYCE
197	16/08/1970	"OUR QUEEN" (MFV) of Douglas (IOM)	SSE x 6-7/ Mod Sea	5h 30m	None	None	Sprang leak off Girdleness. Towed to Aberdeen by HMS MONTROSE and L/boat.	RAMSAY DYCE
198	26/09/1970	"ADORATION" of Kirkcaldy	W x 2/ Slight Sea	0h 37m	None	None	On fire off Crawton Ness. Towed to Stonehaen by MFV. L/boat recalled	RAMSAY DYCE
199	05/09/1971	Yacht "SWORDFISH"	SW x 3/ Slight Sea	1h 40m	None	None	Imagined becalmed, aux engine failed, set off flare.	SOUTHERN AFRICA (RESERVE)
200	12/03/1972	"PREDOMINATE" of Aberdeen	SW x 3/ Choppy	3h 08m	None	None	Engine failed 9nm S of port. L/boat towed to Aberdeen.	RAMSAY DYCE
201	26/04/1972	"ODELLA" of Aberdeen (Yawl)	NNW x 2/ Sl Sea	4h 45m	None	None	Engine failure. Towed to Aberdeen by "DANDARA"	RAMSAY DYCE
202	23/07/1972	Yacht "SWORDFISH"	SE x 2/ Smooth Sea	1h 20m	None	None	Water in fuel off Belhelvie. Towed to port by L/boat.	RAMSAY DYCE
203	14/10/1972	Fournier RF4D Aircraft G-AXJS	Calm (Fog)/ Smooth Sea	3h 05m	1	None	Crashed 6nm SE of port. Searched in company HMS BRINTON & divers. Wreckage found.	HILTON BRIGGS (RESERVE).
204	04/01/1974	"NURZEC" of Gdynia	S x 7-9/ Vy Rough	7h 25m	4	None	Stranded off Murcar. Russian tug's boat capsized in surf. L/boat stood off surf line.	RAMSAY DYCE
205	13/04/1974	"NETTA CROAN" of Leith	Var x 1/	4h 45m	1	12	On fire and out of control off Belhelvie area. Twelve men taken off as helicopter unable.	HILTON BRIGGS (RESERVE)

* RNLI Silver Medal for Coxswain and Mechanic.

No.	Date	Name of Casualty	Wind/ Weather	Duration	Lives Lost	Lives Saved	Brief Service Details	Life-boat
206	07/03/1975	Unknown	SW x 3/ Choppy Sea	3h 05m	None	None	Flares seen off Portlethen. Searched, but nothing found.	RAMSAY DYCE
207	30/12/1975	Unknown	SW x 8/ Rough	1h 55m	None	None	Flares seen off Newtonhill. Searched but nothing found.	RAMSAY DYCE

A stalwart relief — RNLB
"Edith Emille".

No.	Date	Name of Casualty	Wind/ Weather	Duration	Lives Lost	Lives Saved	Brief Service Details	Life-boat
208	29/01/1976	"BEN GULVAIN" of Aberdeen	SSE x 9/ Vy Rough Sea	3h 45m	None	None	Engine failure, stranded N of Don mouth, Crew rescued by BAH helo. L/boat stood by.	RAMSAY DYCE
209	12/03/1976	"KAREMMA" Leith	SE x 1/ Vy Rough Sea	1h 15m	None	5	Steering gear failed in Aberdeen Bay and tug unable to pass tow. L/boat closed and took off crew in three attempts.	RAMSAY DYCE
	* RNLI Bronze Medal for Second Coxswain.							
210	28/07/1976	"WESTERDALE" of Aberdeen	NNW x 4/ Mod Sea	7h 25m	None	None	Leaking & in danger 094° 50nm Girdleness. L/boat put pump on board and escorted to port.	BP FORTIES
211	01/10/1976	"SHERRIFMUIR" Aberdeen	SE x 3/ Rough	3h 11m	None	None	Stranded N of Br of Don. L/boat stood by. Crew walked ashore at low water.	BP FORTIES
212	27/11/1976	Q17 of Cove	SSW x 5/ Choppy	1h 02m	None	2	Engine failure 1nm E of Girdleness. L/boat took crew off and towed vessel to Aberdeen	BP FORTIES
213	03/01/1977	"DAPNE" of Denmark	SW x 2/ Slight Sea	1h 00m	None	None	Engine failure. L/boat took over tow in Bay and into port.	RAMSAY DYCE (RESERVE)
214	01/10/1977	Ditched S-61N helicopter G-BBHN	NW x 7/ Vy Rough Sea	1h 40m	None	None	Ditched 063° 48nm. Survivors picked up by BAH helo. L/boat recalled.	BP FORTIES
215	11/12/1977	Angler washed off rocks	SW x 3/ High Sea	1h 22m	1	None	Immed. S of Gregness CG Stn. Searched, but nothing found. L/boat recalled.	BP FORTIES
216	14/01/1977	Stranded anglers	Varbl/ Slight Sea	0h 50m	None	2	At Girdleness. 'Daughter boat' used.	BP FORTIES
217	31/01/1978	Fishing coble	S x 1/ Rough Sea	1h 05m	None	2	Reported in difficulties 1nm off Cove. L/boat escorted to Cove.	BP FORTIES
218	16/03/1978	"ELWICK BAY" of Kirkwall.	NE x 5/ Mod Sea	5h 02m	None	None	Engine failure 018° 13nm. Escorted to port by L/boat.	BP FORTIES
219	19/03/1978	"HALYCON" of Banff	S x 8/ Vy Rough Sea	3h 42m	None	4	Reported fouled propellor 135* 12nm. L/boat towed to Aberdeen.	BP FORTIES
220	24/08/1978	"MERCURIUS" of Heimstede	W x 2/ Slight Sea		None	None	Crewman with heart attack. L/boat transferred doctor and escorted vessel to port.	JOHN GELLATLY HYNDMAN (RESERVE)
221	01/11/1978	"GEORGE R WOOD" of Aberdeen	S x 7/ Mod Sea	5h 45m	None	None	Engine failure close inshore Collieston. L/boat stood by till tug arrived and esc. to port.	BP FORTIES
222	11/11/1979	"SORJAN" of Denmark	WNW x 3/ Choppy Sea	on passage		None	L/boat on passage Buckie/Abdn. Vessel reported taking water 8nm E Rattray. L/boat to P/head.	BP FORTIES
223	22/02/1980	"NORFOLK SPINNER" of Aberdeen	Calm (Fog)/ Hy Swell	2h 5m	3	None	Stranded root S B/water. L/boat unable close due swell swell, rocks. Daughter boat ineff also.	BP FORTIES
224	31/07/1980	Ditched S-61N helicopter (G-BEID)	Lt Airs S'ly Calm, Fog	7h 20m	None	None	Ditched 082° 17nm. Occupants taken off by helo A/craft towed to Abdn by L/boat.	BP FORTIES
225	08/08/1980	"SHANNON" of Peterhead	SW x 4/ Mod Sea	8h 43m	None	None	Taking water/sinking E x N 26nm. Pumps put on boat L/boat & helo. Towed by MFV to port, escort.	BP FORTIES
226	28/09/1980	Overdue cabin cruiser of Cove	SW x 2/ Smooth	10h 15m	None	None	Searched Cove-S/haven ILB & helo. Cas found I/bervie, towed S/haven by L/boat.	BP FORTIES
227	12/11/1980	"SPEROS" of Leith	NNW x 4-5/ Mod Sea	4h 22m	1	None	Man overboard G/ness 060° x 6nm. Search but no trace.	BP FORTIES
228	17/11/1980	Overdue Aberdeen MFV	SW x 4/ Sl/Choppy Sea	1h 20m	None	None	Not overdue — escorted to Aberdeen.	BP FORTIES
229	19/12/1980 20/12/1980	"ROSS KHARTOUM" of Grimsby	SSE x 7/ High Sea	6h 14m	None	None	Stranded nr Belhelvie. L/boat unable to close. Crew rescued by helo. L/boat stood by.	BP FORTIES
230	14/04/1981	Capsized Abdn ILB	Lt Airs/ Smooth/Sl Surf	0h 50m	None	None	ILB capsized when assisting windsurfer in Bay. Washed ashore. L/boat stood by.	BP FORTIES
231	27/05/1981	"WANDERER" of Aberdeen	NE Airs/ Sl/Smooth Sea	4h 40m	None	None	Reported on fire 18nm ESE. Escorted to port	BP FORTIES
232	12/01/1982	"CONTENDER II" of Kirkcaldy	SSW x 5/ Rough/Mod Sea	6h 28m	None	None	Taking water 10nm ESE. Towed to port "ARTUS" L/boat pump & crew on board to help.	EDITH EMILIE
233	17/02/1982	Student fell off cliffs	E x 4-5/ Mod/Choppy Sea	1h 35m	1	None	S of Cove. Fell 80' hit head on rocks, Searched, with helo, no trace.	BP FORTIES

Returning to station after bi-
weekly exercise 1982.

No.	Date	Name of Casualty	Wind/ Weather	Duration	Lives Lost	Lives Saved	Brief Service Details	Life-boat
234	22/02/1982	"ORION" of Kirkcaldy	SW x 4/ Smooth Sea	0h 55m	None	None	Rept taking water 2½nm SE Tod Head. RGIT escorted to Stonehaven. L/boat recalled.	BP FORTIES
235	04/08/1982	Inflatable Dinghy	L Airs/Fog/ Smooth Sea	2h 05m	None	None	Rept adrift in fog. Nothing found despite search G/ness to Don mouth.	BP FORTIES
236	05/10/1982	"ARDENLEA" of Aberdeen	E x 5/ Rough	2h 30m	None	None	Rept broken down 7nm NE. Towed to port by "SMIT LLOYD 115", esctd by L/boat.	BP FORTIES
237	20/12/1982	Br Cal Bell 214ST helicopter	W x 4/ Sl Sea	0h 20m	None	None	A/craft rep in diff 42nm 062°. L/boat launched on Cox'n initiative. Landed safely, recalled.	BP FORTIES
238	05/11/1983	Motor Boat "GREEN ISLE"	SSE x 4/5 Mod Sea	1h 15m	None	3	Broken down 1.5nm SE Girdleness. Towed to port.	BP FORTIES
239	02/12/1983	Man in sea	Lt Airs Sl/Mod Sea	0h 40m	None	1	Gluesniffer, picked up by safety boat inflatable. Transferred to L/boat. 12 mths probn.	BP FORTIES
240	26/01/1984	"DARSSER ORT" of Hamburg	ESE 8/9 Vy Hy Br Sea	1h 35m	None	None	Rept cargo shifted 13nm St. Escorted into port. Four L/boat crew injured.	EDITH EMILIE (RESERVE)
241	09/02/1984	Not known	Calm/ Smooth	2h 25m	None	None	Flares rep N of Br of Don. Search, nothing found. False alarm with good intent.	EDITH EMILIE (RESERVE)
242	14/04/1984	Windsurfer	SW4/ Choppy	0h 50m	None	1	Blown offshore at Donmouth. Y-boat used to recover from salmon nets.	EDITH EMILIE (RESERVE)
243	08/05/1984	Capsized lobster boat	E3/ Mod Gr Sw	2h 05m	1	None	Capsized off Cove. Search by L/boat, ILB, helo, nothing found.	BP FORTIES
244	29/07/1984	"MEGA STAR" Colombo	S2/ Sl Sea	1h 15m	None	None	Took crewman with facial injuries ashore.	BP FORTIES
245	26/10/84	Persons washed off Promenade	W6/ Sl Swell	2h 5m	1	None	Party skylarking at edge big tide, several in sea. L/boat rec'd 2 handbags & diary.	BP FORTIES
246	27/10/84	Microlight aircraft in sea.	SxW/ Choppy Sw	3h 34m	2	None	M'light a'craft seen ditching off Inverbervie but despite search nothing found.	BP FORTIES
247	29/01/85	"BISHOP BURTON" of Hull	SSW 3 Mod Sea	1h 50m	None	None	Trawler rep'd sinking 26 mls SE Abdn. Crew picked up by RAF helo.	BP FORTIES
248	03/08/85	Surtsey (yacht)	SW 4/6 Mod Sea	11h 15m	None	None	Yacht rep'd rigging failure and engine problems 40 mls E of Abdn. Escorted by L/B to port.	BP FORTIES

RNLB "Southern Africa"
at Pocra Quay on a
blustery day in 1968.

ABERDEEN INSHORE LIFE-BOAT — SERVICE LIST

No.	Date	Name of Casualty	Wind/ Weather	Duration	Lives Lost	Lives Saved	Brief Service Details
001	20/08/1968	Missing girl	SE3 Mod Sw	0h 55m	None	None	Lost in Black Dog dunes area, found safe by helicopter.
002	30/08/1968	MB ''ENSIGN''	SW5-6 Choppy	1h 15m	None	1	Broken down 025° 6nm, towed to Aberdeen by ILB.
003	03/07/1969	MB ''M.A.S.''	S2	0h 55m	None	6	Report of boat burning rags. ILB towed to Aberdeen.
004	14/08/1969	Raft adrift	E2 Mod Sw	1h 35m	None	None	Report of raft adrift Black Dog area. Rescued by coble, latter towed to beach by ILB.
005	19/06/1970	Missing bather	N.A.	3h 00m	1	None	Bather lost in river nr. Victoria Bridge. Body rec by police frogmen, taken ashore by ILB.
006	16/08/1970	MFV ''OUR QUEEN''	SE6-7	N.K.	None	None	Too rough for ILB, became full life-boat service. (See No. 197)
007	24/09/1970	Missing skin diver	Calm Calm	1h 10m	None	None	Report of diver overboard missing, searched, nothing found.
008	18/05/1971	Youth over cliff	SW1-2 Calm	0h 25m	None	1	ILB took casualty back to Aberdeen where ambulance waiting.
009	21/05/1971	Boy stranded in cave	SW2	1h 00m	None	2	Taken off in ILB and brought to Aberdeen.
010	12/06/1971	Boy over cliffs	N3 S1 Sw	1h 15m	1	None	Body taken to Aberdeen by ILB
011	12/08/1971	Persons stranded on cliffs.	E2-3	0h 20m	None	1	Taken off by ILB
012	27/09/1971	Capsized canoe	SE2 S1 Sw	0h 20m	None	None	Near Donmouth, occupant made own way ashore.
013	30/04/1972	Boy over cliffs	S4 Mod Sw	1h 15m	None	None	Recovered by other means.
014	15/08/1972	Boy over cliffs	SW2 Sl Sw	0h 50m	None	None	Hoax call.
015	04/09/1972	Body in gulley	N.K.	1h 10m	1	None	Female body found in gulley nr Cove. Taken to Cove by ILB.
016	05/10/1972	Woman in sea	SW1 Sl Sw	0h 35m	None	1	Attempted suicide. Picked up by ILB. RHS certificates awarded crew members.
017	18/07/1973	Two boys stranded	S3 Sl Sw	0h 25m	None	2	Stranded Gregness, taken off by ILB.
018	26/08/1973	MB ''SKYLARK''	SSW3 Sl Sw	1h 20m	None	3	Adrift ½nm off Donmouth. Towed to Aberdeen by ILB.
019	19/05/1974	Capsized dinghy	S2 Sl Sw	0h 40m	None	None	Capsized off Donmouth, made own way ashore.
020	26/05/1974	Boy stranded on cliffs	SW3 Calm	1h 00m	None	1	Taken off by ILB and brought to Aberdeen
021	04/06/1974	Boy over cliffs	SW1 Calm	0h 20m	None	None	ILB recalled after shore boat uplifted casualty and took to Cove.
022	01/07/1974	Aircraft in sea	NW1-2 Sl Sw	0h 50m	None	None	Aircraft reported in sea 2nm off Girdleness. ILB searched but nothng found.
023	04/08/1976	Bather in trouble	S2 Calm	0h 11m	None	1	ILB reached swimmer off N Pier. Did not require help, but taken on board.
024	19/08/1976	Man in sea	N.K.	N.K.	None	1	Man taken from water and brought ashore to police custody (drunk?).
025	24/05/1977	Man over cliffs	NNE2 Sl Sw	1h 50m	1	None	Fell over cliffs Gregness. ILB took body to Aberdeen.
026	14/07/1977	Missing woman	N.K.	1h 40m	None	None	ILB searched Downies to Cove at request of police, but found nothing.
027	07/04/1981	Boys on sandbank	SSE2-3 Choppy	0h 30m	None	2	Stranded at Donmouth. Taken off by ILB and landed on beach.

Two of a kind — "RNLB BP
Forties" (inboard) — "RNLB
Edith Emile", in Aberdeen
harbour during a relief
changeover.

No.	Date	Name of Casualty	Wind/ Weather	Duration	Lives Lost	Lives Saved	Brief Service Details
028	13/04/1981	Clothes found	SE1-2 Calm	1h 20m	None	None	Searched cliffs Cove area police request following finding of clothes on clifftop.
029	03/08/1981	Flares seen	SSW4 Rough	0h 45m	None	None	Flares reported, ILB searched, but nothing found.
030	29/05/1983	Boy stranded on cliffs	NW3-4 Choppy	1h 20m	None	1	Stranded Gregness, ILB took off and landed on beach in gully. Firemen also taken ashore.
031	20/06/1983	Man fell on rocks	SE2 Smooth	1h 00m	None	None	Angler fell, taken to Aberdeen by ILB.
032	26/06/1983	Inflatable in difficulties	NW4 Sl Sw	0h 11m	None	None	At Balmedie, brought ashore by swimmer. ILB recalled (Station Open Day).
033	30/06/1983	Man in water	NW4 Choppy	0h 19m	None	None	Hoax call — accused fined £100.
034	08/05/1984	Capsized lobster boat	E3 Mod Gr Sw	3h 00m	1	None	Capsized off Cove, ILB searched with shore boats, BP FORTIES, helo. Nothing found.
035	18/06/1984	Recovered body	Calm Calm	2h 10m	None	None	Body from 034 above recovered S of Cove at request police.
036	09/10/1984	Man in sea	NW1-2	0h 55m	None	None	ILB on exercise. Report man at Donmouth. Searched, but found nothing.

ABERDEEN R.N.L.I. LIFE-SAVING APPARATUS — SERVICE LIST

No.	Date	Name of Casualty	Lives Lost	Lives Saved	LSA Unit	Brief Service Details
001	02/06/1931	"Loyal Friend" of Lowestoft	None	11	N Pier	Collided with N Pier. L/boat service No. 016.
002	18/01/1933	"Ben Screel" of Aberdeen	None	10	Torry	Stranded Girdleness. L boat service No. 021
003	25/12/1935	"George Stroud' of Aberdeen	3	1	N Pier	Stranded on N Pier. L/boat service No. 25/12/1935
004	15/04/1945	"Albert Victor" of Faeroes	None	5	N Pier	Stranded on Beach nr Ballroom
005	22/05/1945	HM MTB 2007 (RN vessel)	None	1	Torry	Stranded S side of Nav Channel. L/boat service No. 089.
006	21/01/1946	"Spurs" of Grimsby	None	16	Torry	Stranded in Nav Channel. L/boat service No. 094.
007	23/09/1952	"Loch Lomond"	None	13	N Pier	Stranded on N Pier. L/boat service No. 108

* Both LSA Units closed down mid-1962.

INDEX

(Page numbers cover incidents recorded in the text, numbers in brackets refer to the list of services.)

Index

Index

Chart produced from section of BA chart no. 210 with the
sanction of the Controller, HM stationery office and the
Hydrographer of the Navy.

ABERDEEN TO NEWBURGH

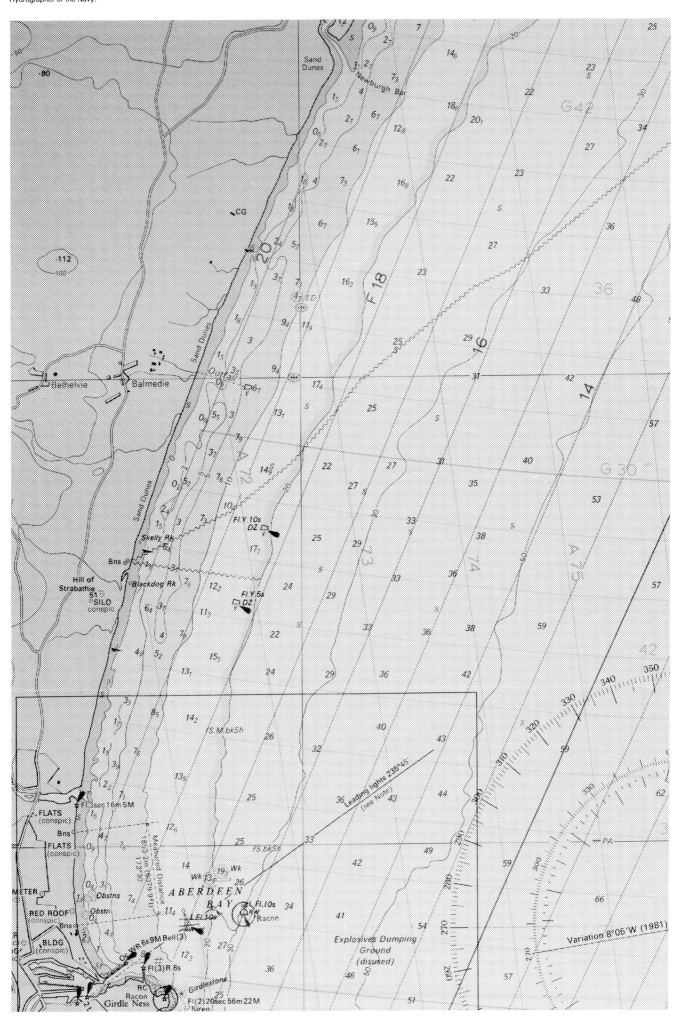

Chart produced from section of BA chart no. 210 with the
sanction of the Controller, HM stationery office and the
Hydrographer of the Navy.

ABERDEEN TO NEWTONHILL

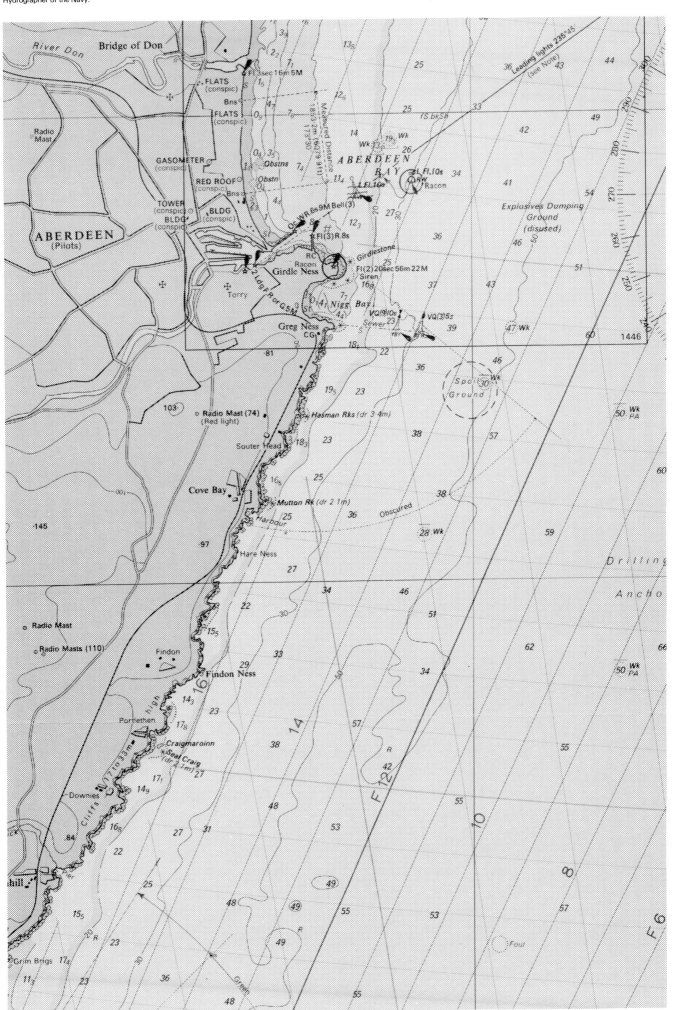

Chart produced from section of BA chart no. 210 with the
sanction of the Controller, HM stationery office and the
Hydrographer of the Navy.

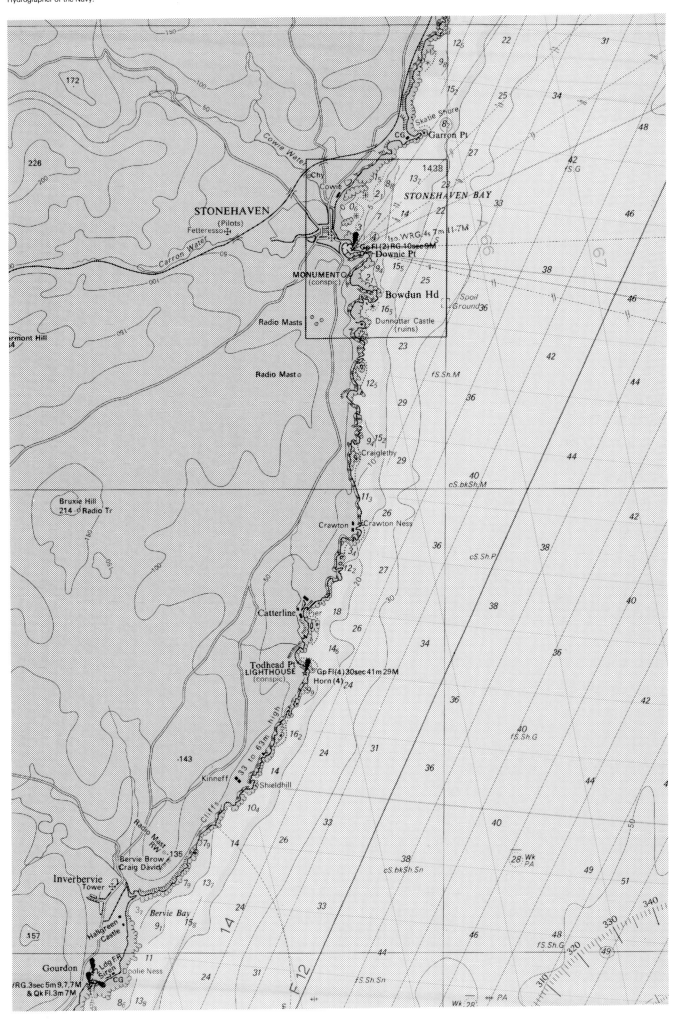